Overthinking Psychology

CRAFTED BY SKRIUWER

Copyright © 2024 by Skriuwer.

All rights reserved. No part of this book may be used or reproduced in any form whatsoever without written permission except in the case of brief quotations in critical articles or reviews.

For more information, contact : **kontakt@skriuwer.com** (www.skriuwer.com)

TABLE OF CONTENTS

CHAPTER 1: UNDERSTANDING OVERTHINKING

- *What overthinking means and why it happens*
- *Difference between healthy thinking and overthinking*
- *Common causes and early warning signs*
- *How recognizing overthinking patterns is the first step*

CHAPTER 2: COMMON TRIGGERS AND SIGNS OF OVERTHINKING

- *Everyday situations that spark anxious thoughts*
- *Physical and emotional signs that signal a spiral*
- *Spotting patterns in your daily life*
- *Strategies for catching overthinking early*

CHAPTER 3: THE PSYCHOLOGY BEHIND THOUGHTS AND EMOTIONS

- *How the brain processes and stores worries*
- *Link between thoughts, feelings, and behavior*
- *Why negative thoughts stick more than positive ones*
- *Turning awareness into action*

CHAPTER 4: HOW OVERTHINKING AFFECTS DAILY LIFE

- *Impact on work, school, and relationships*
- *Role of stress, fatigue, and missed opportunities*
- *Recognizing emotional and physical costs*
- *Breaking unproductive cycles*

CHAPTER 5: BUILDING AWARENESS: RECOGNIZING YOUR TRIGGERS

- *Pinpointing internal vs. external triggers*
- *Using a "trigger map" or diary*
- *Body and mind signals to watch for*
- *Preventing escalation before it starts*

CHAPTER 6: CREATING HELPFUL THOUGHT PATTERNS

- *Shifting from negative to balanced self-talk*
- *Challenging cognitive distortions*
- *Replacing harmful loops with healthy alternatives*
- *Building supportive internal dialogue*

CHAPTER 7: TECHNIQUES TO QUIET THE MIND

- *Practical methods like mindfulness and breathing*
- *Scheduling "worry time" to regain control*
- *Writing or journaling as a release*
- *Using relaxation strategies for daily peace*

CHAPTER 8: DEVELOPING EMOTIONAL RESILIENCE

- *Understanding and bouncing back from setbacks*
- *Learning to accept failure without self-blame*
- *Building coping skills for stress*
- *Cultivating a stronger, calmer mindset*

CHAPTER 9: HABITS AND ROUTINES FOR MENTAL CLARITY

- *Designing morning and evening routines*
- *Time-blocking and task prioritization*
- *Avoiding burnout through planned downtime*
- *Keeping your daily life structured yet flexible*

CHAPTER 10: THE ROLE OF PHYSICAL HEALTH IN REDUCING OVERTHINKING

- *Connecting diet, exercise, and sleep to mental calm*
- *How stress hormones affect worrying*
- *Practical tips for balanced nutrition and rest*
- *Creating healthier daily patterns*

CHAPTER 11: DEALING WITH ANXIETY AND STRESS

- *Short-term tools like deep breathing and grounding*
- *Long-term approaches, including CBT techniques*
- *Facing daily stressors effectively*
- *Recognizing when anxiety points to bigger issues*

CHAPTER 12: MINDFULNESS AND FOCUS STRATEGIES

- *Staying present to disrupt negative loops*
- *Formal meditation vs. everyday mindfulness*
- *Concentration methods for work or study*
- *Minimizing digital overload and distractions*

CHAPTER 13: COMMUNICATION SKILLS TO SHARE AND UNBURDEN

- *Power of talking about worries and reducing isolation*
- *Active listening and respectful conflict resolution*
- *Overcoming fear of judgment or burdening others*
- *Creating open, honest dialogue in relationships*

CHAPTER 14: OVERCOMING NEGATIVE SELF-TALK

- *Identifying common forms of harsh inner dialogue*
- *Replacing destructive thoughts with supportive ones*
- *Building healthier mental narratives*
- *Finding self-compassion in daily life*

CHAPTER 15: COPING WITH PERFECTIONISM AND FEAR OF FAILURE

- *Recognizing impossible standards that fuel worry*
- *Practical steps to challenge perfectionistic habits*
- *Reframing failure as part of growth*
- *Strategies to reduce performance-related anxiety*

CHAPTER 16: SETTING REALISTIC GOALS AND PLANS

- *How clarity in goals cuts down on overthinking*
- *Using SMART (Specific, Measurable, Achievable, Relevant, Time-bound) structure*
- *Breaking big dreams into smaller tasks*
- *Balancing ambition with practicality*

CHAPTER 17: BUILDING CONFIDENCE AND SELF-ESTEEM

- *Why self-worth safeguards against anxious thoughts*
- *Overcoming self-doubt and negative beliefs*
- *Incremental skill-building for lasting competence*
- *Developing a kinder view of yourself*

CHAPTER 18: USING SUPPORT SYSTEMS AND PROFESSIONAL HELP

- *Finding friends, family, and group support*
- *Deciding when therapy or counseling is needed*
- *Types of mental health professionals*
- *Normalizing the process of seeking assistance*

CHAPTER 19: LONG-TERM STRATEGIES FOR A BALANCED MIND

- *Sustaining positive routines over time*
- *Staying resilient through life changes and stress*
- *Refining your coping methods as you grow*
- *Periodic reviews to catch relapses early*

CHAPTER 20: MOVING FORWARD WITH A CLEAR MIND

- *Summarizing core lessons and strategies*
- *Maintaining progress without backsliding*
- *Creating a personal roadmap for the future*
- *Stepping confidently into each new chapter of life*

Chapter 1: Understanding Overthinking

Introduction

Overthinking is when we spend too much time stuck in our thoughts. We may feel like our minds will not stop racing. It can feel like a hamster running on a wheel, never taking a break. Sometimes, overthinking can be about mistakes we made in the past. Other times, it can be about worries for the future. This first chapter will help you see why overthinking happens, what it looks like, and why it can be harmful if not handled. The goal is to lay the groundwork so you can recognize overthinking in your life and make sense of it.

What Is Overthinking?

Overthinking means thinking about something more than necessary. For example, imagine you make a small mistake at work or school. You start replaying it in your mind again and again, wondering if people are judging you. Even if it was a small slip, you dwell on it for hours or days. Overthinking is not just being careful or thorough; it is going beyond what is helpful until it causes stress.

When we overthink, our minds loop the same worries, fears, or doubts. Some people overthink about things that happened already, while others overthink about what might happen soon. This can cause restless nights, physical tension, and emotional discomfort. It is important to know that overthinking does not solve problems. Instead, it often makes them feel bigger and more confusing.

The Difference Between Overthinking and Healthy Thinking

Healthy thinking helps us plan or understand a situation. For example, if you have a test coming up, it makes sense to think about what you need to study. You might make a schedule and practice each subject. This is logical and leads to action. On the other hand, overthinking would be sitting for hours, feeling panicked about failing, imagining worst-case scenarios, and never getting started on actual studying.

Healthy thinking leads to solutions or steps. Overthinking leads to more worry and less action. A good way to see the difference is to ask yourself, "Am I doing something useful with my thoughts, or am I just spinning my wheels?" If you feel stuck and anxious, you might be overthinking.

Why Do People Overthink?

People overthink for various reasons. Sometimes it can be related to stress from work, school, or relationships. Other times, it might come from a fear of making mistakes. If someone had a bad experience in the past, they might think too hard about not letting it happen again. Here are a few common reasons:

1. **Fear of Failure**: People may overthink because they want everything to go perfectly. They do not want to fail or disappoint others. So, they try to anticipate all possible problems, which can become overwhelming.
2. **Worry About the Future**: Some individuals focus on the "what ifs" of tomorrow. They might wonder, "What if I lose my job?" or "What if people do not like what I do?" This constant worry can lead to sleepless nights.
3. **Past Mistakes**: Others dwell on past experiences, replaying them repeatedly. They might think, "I wish I had done it differently," or "Why did I say that?" They get stuck trying to rewrite history in their minds, which is not possible.
4. **Seeking Approval**: When people want acceptance from friends, family, or peers, they might overanalyze everything they do or say. They wonder if they offended someone or if they seemed awkward, leading to excessive thinking.
5. **High Stress Lifestyle**: Busy schedules and never-ending tasks can keep the mind on full alert. When the brain does not get a break, it can fall into overthinking patterns even at night when trying to sleep.

How Overthinking Feels

Overthinking can feel like a heavy weight in your head. You might wake up feeling tired because your mind was working overtime. Sometimes, you know you are worrying too much, but you cannot stop. You might try to distract yourself by watching TV or playing a game, but as soon as it is quiet, the thoughts flood back in. It can feel like you have no control over your own head.

Physically, overthinking can cause tight muscles, headaches, an upset stomach, or difficulty sleeping. Emotionally, it can lead to anxiety, sadness, or frustration. You might notice your heart beating faster when you think about a scary or upsetting scenario. Overall, your body reacts to your thoughts, and your mind stays busy, creating a cycle that feels difficult to break.

The Cost of Overthinking

It might seem harmless to think a lot. After all, many people believe thinking is always good. But too much thinking without action or resolution can be damaging. Here are some ways overthinking can cost you:

1. **Lost Time**: You could spend hours or days stuck in your head. This is time that could be used for fun activities, learning new skills, or resting.
2. **Missed Opportunities**: Some people wait too long to make decisions because they are overthinking. They might miss chances to try something new or take on a new project.
3. **Strained Relationships**: Overthinking can make you suspicious or anxious around friends and family. You might assume they are upset with you, even if they are not, because you are reading too deeply into small things.
4. **Emotional Exhaustion**: Constant worry and replaying the same thoughts is tiring. You could feel drained, which can affect your motivation and joy in life.
5. **Increased Stress**: Overthinking often builds up stress hormones in the body. High stress can lead to health problems if it continues for a long time.

Overthinking vs. Analytical Thinking

It is important to understand that being thoughtful is not the same as overthinking. Analytical thinking is when you gather facts, look at the big picture, and then make logical conclusions. You do not dwell on the same fear repeatedly. Instead, you examine the situation and form a plan.

Overthinking is when you keep getting stuck in doubt or fear. You might say, "But what if it goes wrong?" or "What if I forgot something important?" over and over. Analytical thinking respects the need to consider risks, but it also recognizes when you have enough information to act.

Understanding the Overthinking Cycle

One way to see overthinking is as a cycle. First, you encounter a trigger. A trigger can be an event, a memory, or a worry. Next, you respond with anxiety or fear, which leads to more thoughts about that topic. You might try to "fix" it by thinking harder. Instead of solving anything, you increase your anxiety. That anxiety then fuels more overthinking, creating a loop.

Example: You get a text from your boss or teacher that says, "We need to talk tomorrow." You start thinking, "Is this about something I did wrong?" Then you recall every possible mistake from the past week. You imagine the worst case, like getting fired or failing a class. Your mind keeps going until you are in full panic. By the time you meet your boss or teacher, you are exhausted—and sometimes you find out it was not anything serious at all.

Early Signs You Might Be Overthinking

It helps to notice the first signs before your mind goes into overdrive. Here are some warning signals:

1. **Difficulty Letting Go**: You cannot stop thinking about a certain event or worry, even if it happened a long time ago.
2. **Constant "What If" Questions**: You find yourself frequently asking, "What if this happens?" or "What if that doesn't work out?"

3. **Trouble Sleeping**: Your mind feels too busy to rest, and you lie awake with racing thoughts.
4. **Second-Guessing Everything**: Even small decisions become huge challenges. You doubt your choices and fear making the wrong move.
5. **Seeking Excessive Reassurance**: You keep asking people around you, "Do you think I did the right thing?" or "Are you sure I didn't upset anyone?"

If these sound familiar, you might be a person who tends to overthink. Recognizing this pattern is a strong first step because it allows you to try new ways of handling your thoughts.

How Overthinking Impacts Daily Life

Overthinking can sneak into every corner of your life:

- **Work or School**: You may spend too much time preparing for a task, worrying if it's good enough. This can lead to missed deadlines because you spent more time worrying than working.
- **Relationships**: Overthinking about what someone said or how they said it can cause misunderstandings. Instead of asking for clarity, you might assume they are angry with you or do not value you.
- **Personal Goals**: You could delay setting goals because you are scared to fail. Overthinking might convince you that you will not succeed, so you do not even try.
- **Mental Health**: Overthinking drains mental energy, leaving you too tired to enjoy activities or social events. You might isolate yourself or become irritable with friends and family.

Breaking the Stigma

Some people believe that if you are an overthinker, it is your fault. They might say things like, "Just relax," or "Stop thinking so much." This advice usually does not help. Overthinking can become a habit. It might be tied to deeper anxiety issues or past traumas. Blaming someone for overthinking does not fix it. Instead, we need to understand it as a pattern that can be changed with patience, self-awareness, and the right tools.

Real-Life Example: Sarah's Story

Sarah was a high school student who worried a lot about her grades. She felt pressure from her parents to do well. Each time she got less than a perfect score on a test, she would replay the questions in her head and blame herself for every mistake. Her friends noticed she was always tense. She often asked them, "Do you think I'm dumb for missing that question?"

This constant worry hurt Sarah's focus in class. She spent more time thinking about the past tests than preparing for upcoming ones. Eventually, Sarah realized this pattern was stopping her from enjoying school and learning. She decided to talk to a school counselor, who explained that she was overthinking. With time, Sarah learned techniques to manage her thoughts, like writing them down in a journal. This helped her see the worries more clearly, and she could address them step by step.

Self-Awareness: The Key to Understanding

The first real step to deal with overthinking is self-awareness. This means being able to say, "Yes, I can see that I am stuck in my thoughts right now." It might be helpful to pause and notice any physical tension, like tightened shoulders or a clenched jaw. By identifying when you start overthinking, you can stop it earlier.

Ways to Build Self-Awareness

- **Journaling**: Write down your worries, questions, and feelings. Seeing them on paper can help you notice patterns.
- **Body Scan**: Close your eyes for a moment and mentally scan from your head to your toes, checking how each part feels. Are you tense anywhere? Do you feel anxious in your stomach? Recognizing these sensations can alert you to overthinking.
- **Mindful Breathing**: Take a few deep breaths, paying attention to how the air moves in and out. This pulls you back into the present and helps you see if you are lost in thoughts about the past or future.

Differences Among Individuals

Not everyone experiences overthinking in the same way. Some people might have short bursts of overthinking, while others might struggle with it for longer periods. Your personality plays a role, too. People who are naturally reflective may find it harder to shut off their minds. Life experiences also shape how we think. If you grew up with a lot of criticism or sudden changes, you might be more prone to double-checking everything in your head.

Understanding that overthinking can be part of different personality types helps remove shame. It is not a sign of weakness or failure. It is just a pattern that can be improved once you recognize it and decide to make changes.

Overthinking in Today's World

Modern life is fast. With technology, we have constant updates. Social media can make us compare our lives to others. We might overthink our posts, photos, or opinions online. We might worry if someone does not "like" our posts or if people misunderstand us. Online communication can also lack the tone and body language we get in face-to-face conversations, leading to misunderstandings that spark more overthinking.

At school or work, many people feel pressure to perform at a high level, as if they can never make mistakes. This creates a perfect environment for overthinking. We worry about how we measure up, whether we are meeting expectations, and if we are falling behind our peers.

The Importance of Recognizing Overthinking Early

Overthinking does not go away on its own. The longer we let it control our thoughts, the more it becomes a habit. Imagine you have a path in the forest that you walk daily. Over time, that path becomes clearer and easier to walk. Overthinking is like a path in your brain: the more you use it, the more natural it feels to return to it.

If you notice your overthinking early, you can learn strategies to break out of it. This may include changing your daily routine, talking to someone you trust, or practicing relaxation methods. The earlier you catch yourself overthinking, the quicker you can shift your thoughts to something more productive.

When Overthinking Might Point to Other Issues

Sometimes, overthinking is a sign of deeper problems. People with anxiety disorders, depression, or trauma history might find it especially hard to control their thoughts. If overthinking is severe, it may be wise to seek help from a professional, like a therapist or counselor. They can help you work through not just the habit of overthinking, but also the root causes behind it.

Steps Toward Change

1. **Admit the Problem**: Say to yourself, "I recognize that I overthink. It causes me stress, and I want to do better."
2. **Learn About the Issue**: You are reading this book, which is a good start. You can also watch videos or read articles about overthinking to gather more insights.
3. **Experiment with Techniques**: Try different methods like journaling, breathing exercises, or mindfulness to see what helps calm your thoughts.
4. **Reflect and Adjust**: Notice what works and what does not. Overthinking is a habit, and changing habits takes trial and error.
5. **Keep Practicing**: Even if you slip back into overthinking, do not be hard on yourself. Change takes time. Keep practicing, and it will become easier.

Conclusion

Overthinking is more than just thinking a lot. It is a pattern that can stop you from moving forward and living a balanced life. We have covered what overthinking is, why it happens, and how it can affect you. Recognizing this pattern is the first big step in handling it. In the next chapters, we will look at common triggers and signs, the psychology behind thoughts and emotions, and deeper methods to manage and quiet the mind. By the end of this book, you will have a wide range of tools to help you avoid falling into the trap of overthinking. You will learn how to replace unhelpful thoughts with clearer, more productive ones, leading to a calmer, more focused life.

Chapter 2: Common Triggers and Signs of Overthinking

Introduction

We have learned what overthinking is and how it affects our lives. Now, let us dive deeper into the triggers and signs that set off this chain of too much thinking. A "trigger" is something that starts or worsens your overthinking. It could be an event, a person's words, a memory, or even a feeling. By learning your triggers, you can catch yourself earlier in the process. This will help you respond in a healthier way, rather than letting your thoughts run wild.

In this chapter, we will discuss how to identify what makes you overthink, common triggers people face, and the main signs that show up when overthinking takes over. This knowledge can act like a compass, guiding you toward solutions.

What Is a Trigger?

A trigger is anything that prompts a strong emotional or mental reaction. It might be a small detail that other people overlook. For instance, a simple text message that says, "We need to talk," could be a trigger if you fear confrontation. Another example might be seeing someone post about their success on social media if you often compare yourself to others. Triggers make us feel uneasy, threatened, or uncertain, which leads to overthinking in an attempt to make sense of those feelings.

Why Identifying Triggers Is Important

- **Early Intervention**: If you can name a trigger, you can take steps to calm yourself before the overthinking cycle intensifies.
- **Self-Understanding**: You learn more about your worries and fears, which can give you insight into what is going on underneath the surface.

- **Clearer Communication**: When you know your triggers, you can explain them to friends or family. They can help you avoid unnecessary stress or misunderstandings.

Common Types of Triggers

1. Social Triggers

These might include gatherings, parties, or even going to school or work where you must interact with many people. If you are shy or have social anxiety, you could overthink your every move, wondering if people are judging you. A friendly joke from someone might be taken personally if you are prone to thinking it hides deeper meaning. Even simple social situations can become draining for an overthinker who imagines all the possible negative outcomes.

2. Performance Triggers

At work or school, performance triggers can arise from tests, presentations, or performance reviews. If you are afraid of failure or criticism, these situations might spark overthinking. You might spend hours rehearsing every possible question you could be asked, or replaying a presentation in your mind long after it is over. Instead of focusing on learning and growing, you might focus on avoiding mistakes, which only adds pressure and anxiety.

3. Emotional Triggers

Sometimes, our own feelings can trigger overthinking. Sadness, anger, or fear might make you overanalyze your thoughts or actions, trying to figure out "why" you feel that way. For example, if you feel guilty about something, you may keep returning to that guilt, dissecting every moment that led up to it. Emotional triggers are powerful because they tap into our basic need for emotional safety and stability.

4. Relationship Triggers

Issues with friends, family, or romantic partners can set off a storm of overthinking. Perhaps you had a disagreement with a friend, and now you are replaying each word you said. You wonder if they are still angry or if they misunderstood you. You might check your phone often to see if they have replied to your messages. Overthinking in relationships can make small problems grow bigger, as you might assume the worst before finding out the facts.

5. Comparison Triggers

Social media often magnifies comparison triggers. You see people posting about new jobs, new houses, or fun vacations. If you feel behind in life or unhappy with your current situation, you could overthink your own choices and achievements. You might think, "Should I be farther along than I am?" or "Am I doing enough with my life?" This comparison trap can quickly spiral into negative self-talk.

6. Unexpected Changes

Sudden changes—like a job loss, a shift in living arrangements, or even an unexpected exam—can flip your world upside down. When you do not have time to prepare, you may feel uncertain, and that uncertainty triggers overthinking. You want to regain control, so you try to predict all outcomes. Unfortunately, this can lead to endless worrying instead of proactive planning.

7. Health Triggers

Fears about health, whether it is your own or a loved one's, can create constant worry. A small symptom can lead to googling health conditions, imagining worst-case scenarios, and losing sleep. If you overthink about health issues, you might spend hours reading online articles, fueling your fears rather than getting a proper medical opinion.

How to Spot a Trigger in Real Life

Spotting a trigger is about noticing your emotional and physical reactions. When something happens and you feel your heart rate jump, or you notice tension in your shoulders, ask yourself, "What just happened?" Maybe someone made a comment that reminded you of a past failure. That could be a trigger. Or you read a social media post that made you feel inadequate. Recognizing the moment you start feeling anxious or uneasy is key to identifying triggers.

Practical Tips

- **Keep a Trigger Diary**: Write down when you feel an overthinking episode coming on. Note the date, time, situation, and who you were with, as well as your thoughts and feelings. Over time, patterns may emerge.
- **Ask a Trusted Person**: Sometimes others notice patterns we do not. Ask a friend, family member, or counselor if they see anything that often upsets you or leads you to dwell on worries.
- **Reflect on the Past**: Look at major events or moments in your life where you started overthinking. What was happening then? Understanding past triggers can help you be ready when similar events happen again.

Signs of Overthinking

Learning the signs of overthinking will help you catch yourself before you sink too deep into it. Here are clear markers:

1. **Repeating Thoughts**: If you keep revisiting the same concern or memory, that's a sign. You might not even notice time passing as your mind loops the same content.
2. **Over-Planning**: While planning is healthy, over-planning involves getting stuck in too many details. You might create countless to-do lists but never start any task because you are afraid of not doing it right.
3. **Tension and Stress**: Physical signs like headaches, stiff neck, or upset stomach can signal that you are worrying too much. Emotions like anxiety, irritability, or sadness can also be big indicators.
4. **Seeking Constant Approval**: If you feel unsure about your decisions and always ask others for reassurance, it may mean you are overthinking. You do not trust your own judgment, so you look for outside opinions to confirm you are doing "the right thing."
5. **Difficulty Focusing**: Overthinking fills your mind with random worries, which can make it hard to concentrate on what is in front of you. Tasks may take longer because your mind is not fully present.
6. **Procrastination**: You might put off tasks because you are too worried about how to start or how they might go. You think, "What if I can't do it well?" So you delay taking action.

7. **Worst-Case Scenarios**: A big sign is immediately jumping to the worst possible outcome. Even a small problem can become a huge catastrophe in your mind.

Early Physical Signs

The body often warns you before your mind registers it. Some physical signs you might notice:

- **Rapid Heartbeat**: Your heart starts pounding for no clear reason.
- **Clenched Jaw or Fists**: You might catch yourself tensing your jaw muscles or making a fist subconsciously.
- **Restlessness**: You cannot sit still. Your legs bounce, or you fidget with your hands because of pent-up nervous energy.
- **Sweaty Palms**: This can happen when you are anxious or worried.
- **Trouble Breathing Deeply**: You may start taking short, shallow breaths without noticing.

Connecting Triggers with Signs: A Real-Life Example

Let's consider David, who experiences a trigger and the signs that follow:

Trigger: David gets a text from his boss: "We need to talk about your latest report."

- **Initial Thought**: "Did I mess up the report?"
- **Physical Signs**: His heart starts beating faster, and his breathing becomes shallow.
- **Emotional Signs**: He feels a wave of anxiety.
- **Behavioral Reaction**: He rereads his report multiple times, trying to spot errors. He imagines all the ways his boss might be upset with him.
- **Overthinking Loop**: David keeps thinking, "I should have spent more time on the data. Maybe I didn't do enough research. What if this ruins my reputation at work?"

Because of this pattern, David might lose sleep, feel irritable with friends or family, and be unable to relax. All of these are clear signs he is overthinking due to that single text message trigger.

How Overthinking and Triggers Interact

Triggers set off the first spark, but it is the overthinking pattern that feeds the fire. Overthinking might last minutes, hours, or days after the trigger is gone. You can compare it to accidentally stepping on the gas pedal of a car. The trigger is the initial push, and overthinking is you keeping your foot pressed down even when you do not need to move that fast. Recognizing when a trigger causes you to "press the gas" is a major step toward letting go of the pedal.

Why Some People Are More Sensitive to Triggers

Certain people might be more sensitive to triggers due to their personality, experiences, or environment. For instance, if you grew up in a home where mistakes were heavily criticized, you might be more triggered by any sign of disapproval. Or if you have faced unpredictable events (like sudden losses or chaotic life changes), you might develop a strong need for control, and anything uncertain becomes a trigger.

Brain and Emotional Health

Stress and anxiety levels can also change how sensitive you are. When you are already stressed or tired, a small comment can feel huge. When you are well-rested and relaxed, the same comment might not bother you at all. This is why it is important to take care of your emotional health. Activities like exercise, mindfulness, and proper sleep can help you become less reactive to potential triggers.

Avoiding Repetition and Recognizing Patterns

When learning about triggers and signs, it is easy to get stuck in the cycle of simply labeling them. But to move forward, you need to use this knowledge. Once you know your biggest triggers, you can plan in advance how to handle them. For example, if you know that social situations trigger you, prepare some calming strategies to use before and after an event. This can help break the overthinking loop.

Immediate Steps When You Face a Trigger

1. **Pause and Breathe**: Take a few slow, deep breaths. This helps calm your body and mind.
2. **Identify the Trigger**: Say to yourself, "I see that this situation is making me anxious because it reminds me of X." Just naming it can lessen its power.
3. **Check the Facts**: Ask yourself if there is real evidence for your worry. For instance, does your boss's message really mean trouble, or could it be something else?
4. **Focus on the Present**: Try to stay grounded in what is happening now, rather than diving into "what if" scenarios about the past or future.
5. **Reach Out**: If you are feeling overwhelmed, talk to someone you trust or write down your thoughts in a notebook.

Developing Healthy Boundaries

Sometimes, overthinking is triggered because we let too many external factors influence our mental space. Developing healthy boundaries means knowing when to step back from social media, certain people, or stressful tasks. For instance, if seeing people brag online triggers your self-doubt, limit your social media time. If a friend always criticizes you, let them know how their behavior makes you feel or consider limiting your time with them if possible.

Boundaries with Yourself

Setting boundaries is not only for dealing with others. You also need boundaries with your own thoughts. If you notice you are starting to replay a conversation endlessly, set a timer for five minutes. Use that time to let your mind run. When the timer goes off, gently tell yourself to move on to another activity. This "worry window" approach can help you keep overthinking in check.

Long-Term Management

Understanding triggers and signs is a foundational step, but real change requires consistent effort. Over time, you might see certain triggers lose their intensity. You might learn that you can handle the fear of giving a speech once you have prepared enough and practiced relaxation. Or you might realize that a friend's teasing is not personal, allowing you to let go of the negativity more easily.

Creating a Plan

Try creating a personal plan for the triggers you face most. Write them down and list ways you can respond. For example:

Trigger: Getting a message from your boss.

- **Plan**:
    1. Read the message carefully.
    2. Breathe deeply, reminding yourself not to jump to conclusions.
    3. If needed, send a short reply to clarify the nature of the meeting.
    4. Distract yourself with a productive task until you meet with the boss.

This way, when a trigger arises, you have a clear, practiced path to follow, rather than letting your mind wander into endless worries.

When to Seek Help

Sometimes, despite learning about triggers and signs, overthinking can remain strong. If overthinking leads to severe stress, impacts your work or school, or strains important relationships, seeking professional help can be a lifesaver. Therapists, counselors, or support groups can offer new perspectives and tools that you might not find on your own. There is no shame in needing help. Overthinking is a habit many people struggle with, and support can speed up the process of change.

Conclusion

Triggers are the sparks that light the fire of overthinking. Knowing what they are and how to recognize them early can save you from deep worry. The signs of overthinking—like repeating thoughts, muscle tension, and constant self-doubt—act as warnings that you need to slow down and find balance. By keeping track of triggers and learning how to handle them, you give yourself a chance to break the cycle before it fully takes over.

In the following chapters, we will explore the inner workings of our minds, how thoughts and emotions connect, and more strategies for dealing with overthinking. By building on what you learned here, you will be able to put together a toolbox of skills to manage triggers, calm your mind, and keep overthinking in check. The journey is not always simple, but with each step, you get closer to finding peace, focus, and confidence in your day-to-day life.

Chapter 3: The Psychology Behind Thoughts and Emotions

Introduction

Our thoughts and emotions are closely linked. When we talk about overthinking, we are really talking about getting stuck in certain types of thoughts that trigger strong feelings, such as worry, fear, or sadness. This chapter will explore some basic psychology to help you see how thoughts form, how emotions develop, and why our minds hold on to certain ideas. By understanding how the mind works, you can better address your overthinking habits and build healthier thought patterns.

How the Brain Processes Thoughts

The human brain is a complex organ made up of billions of nerve cells. While it is far too detailed for us to cover every part, there are a few key areas and processes worth understanding:

1. **Prefrontal Cortex**: This is often linked with decision-making, planning, and self-control. When you are trying to analyze a problem or plan an event, you use this part of your brain. It also helps you stop and think before acting.
2. **Limbic System**: This system includes the amygdala and the hippocampus. The amygdala is like an alarm that reacts to threats or strong emotions (like fear or anger). The hippocampus deals with forming memories. When something scares you or stresses you out, your amygdala might become very active, and your hippocampus might store that experience in a way that makes it easy to recall later.
3. **Neural Pathways**: Whenever you repeat a thought or action, you strengthen certain neural pathways in your brain. Think of a trail in the woods that becomes clearer each time someone walks on it. Overthinking can become a well-worn trail if you do it frequently.

When you overthink, your brain devotes a lot of energy to repeating certain worries, fears, or regrets. This can trigger your limbic system, making your emotional response even stronger, which in turn sends more signals to keep thinking about the issue. It becomes a loop: thoughts feed emotions, which feed more thoughts.

Why Negative Thoughts Stick

Many people notice that negative thoughts seem to "stick" more strongly than positive ones. There is a psychological reason for this: our brains have a bias called the "negativity bias." In simple terms, our ancestors had to pay close attention to threats (like predators or dangerous situations) to survive. If a person overlooked a threat, they might not live another day. Because of this, our brains are wired to notice and remember negative events more strongly.

In modern life, this ancient survival system can cause us to focus on or replay any bad event, real or imagined. That is why a small criticism can stick in your mind longer than five compliments. And if you are an overthinker, your mind might replay that criticism even more, making it seem bigger than it really is.

Emotions as Signals

Emotions are not just random feelings; they can be seen as signals or messengers. Fear tells you that there might be danger. Sadness can tell you that you lost something important. Anger might show that you feel mistreated. Happiness often signals that you like what is happening and want more of it.

However, sometimes our emotion signals get distorted. For instance, a small fear can grow into anxiety if we keep feeding the worry. Emotions can also linger longer than needed. Overthinkers might take a brief fear and hold on to it, analyzing it over and over, until it no longer matches reality.

Learning that emotions are signals rather than facts can help you see them more clearly. Think of it like a traffic light: a red light means stop, but it doesn't mean you will never get to drive again. In the same way, a feeling of fear does not mean you will always be in danger—sometimes it is just a momentary signal that you can acknowledge and then let pass.

Beliefs and Core Thoughts

Our beliefs act like filters through which we see the world. A belief is a strong conviction about yourself, others, or life in general. For example, if you believe "I am not good enough," you might overthink any small mistake to prove that belief right. On the other hand, if you believe "I can handle challenges," you might face failures or setbacks without dwelling on them too long.

How Beliefs Form

- **Early Experiences**: What you learned as a child can shape how you see yourself. If you grew up in an environment where mistakes were harshly criticized, you might carry the belief that any failure is a sign of personal weakness.
- **Repeated Messages**: If people around you often say, "You're lazy," or "You always mess up," you might take these messages to heart. Over time, they become part of your identity.
- **Society and Culture**: Media, culture, and societal norms can also create beliefs. A person might adopt the idea that they must always appear perfect to gain acceptance.

Impact of Beliefs on Overthinking

When a thought or event challenges a strong belief, you might overthink to protect that belief. For example, if you see yourself as unworthy, and someone compliments your work, you could overthink that compliment until you find a reason to dismiss it. "They're just being nice" or "They don't really mean it." Understanding that beliefs can drive overthinking can help you question whether those beliefs are actually true.

The Role of Hormones and Stress

When you are stressed, your body releases hormones like cortisol and adrenaline. These hormones were designed to help humans react to threats quickly: your heart rate goes up, your senses become sharper, and you feel that surge of energy. This "fight or flight" response is helpful in real danger, like avoiding a speeding car.

However, when the threat is imagined or mostly emotional—like a fear of being judged in a presentation—your body can still flood you with stress hormones. If you keep overthinking negative scenarios, your body remains in a high state of alert, leading to:

- Sleeplessness
- Tense muscles
- Headaches
- Digestive issues
- Weakened immune system

Over time, high stress can also contribute to anxiety and depression. Recognizing when you are stuck in a stress loop because of your thoughts is key to breaking free. Techniques like deep breathing, meditation, or exercise can help reduce the buildup of stress hormones and bring your body and mind back into balance.

Conscious vs. Subconscious Mind

It may help to picture your mind as having two main levels: the conscious mind and the subconscious mind.

1. **Conscious Mind**: This is what you are aware of at any given moment. It is the voice that talks in your head and thinks through problems. Overthinking happens mostly at the conscious level— you are actively engaging with thoughts.
2. **Subconscious Mind**: This is deeper. It holds habits, long-term memories, and automatic reactions. For instance, when you drive on a familiar road and do not have to think about each turn, that is your subconscious mind at work. Negative beliefs and triggers can also hide in this area, guiding how you respond to stress.

Why does this matter? Because sometimes you consciously know that a worry is overblown ("Logically, I know I'll be fine"), yet you still feel anxious. This is because your subconscious mind might be holding onto fear from past experiences. Working through deep-rooted fears and beliefs can help bridge the gap between what you logically know and what you emotionally feel.

How Thoughts Turn Into Emotions

A simplified way to see this process is:

1. **Trigger**: Something happens—a situation, a memory, or even a random thought.
2. **Interpretation**: You give meaning to what happened. For example, if your friend is late, you might think, "They don't value my time."
3. **Emotional Response**: Based on that meaning, you feel a certain emotion (anger, sadness, worry).
4. **Physical Reaction**: Your body responds to the emotion with changes like a faster heart rate or tense muscles.
5. **Behavior**: You act (or sometimes do nothing) based on the emotion. In an overthinking loop, this might mean you sit and dwell on the situation for hours.

Many times, we jump from trigger directly to emotion without noticing the interpretation. Overthinkers often have the same interpretation patterns that lead them to negative emotions. By slowing down and asking, "How am I interpreting this?" you can break the cycle.

Emotional Regulation and the Brain

Emotional regulation is your ability to calm down or cheer up as needed. People who struggle with overthinking might also struggle with emotional regulation because they feel trapped by thoughts that keep their emotions stirred up. The brain regions responsible for self-control (like the prefrontal cortex) and emotional processing (like the amygdala) need to communicate properly. When you practice skills like mindfulness, journaling, or talking out your worries, you strengthen the connection between these areas, making it easier to regulate your emotions.

Understanding Triggers on a Deeper Level

In the previous chapter, we looked at triggers that spark overthinking. Psychologically, triggers often tap into old hurts or beliefs. For example, if you were teased as a child for being awkward, a minor joke from a coworker now might feel like a personal attack. Your brain ties the present event to a painful past memory. This can happen so quickly that you do not realize the link consciously, but your emotions flare up anyway.

Healing Old Wounds

Part of stopping overthinking is healing these old emotional wounds. This might involve therapy or self-help methods where you revisit those past experiences and update the meaning you assigned to them. For instance, you might realize that the teasing you faced as a child does not define you today. Changing how you see old events can lessen their ability to trigger you now.

Cognitive Distortions

Cognitive distortions are biased ways of thinking that can lead you into overthinking spirals. Some common ones include:

1. **All-or-Nothing Thinking**: Viewing situations as entirely good or bad.
2. **Overgeneralization**: Making a broad assumption based on one event ("I failed this test, so I'm bad at everything.").
3. **Catastrophizing**: Expecting the worst possible outcome every time.
4. **Personalization**: Taking things personally that might have nothing to do with you.
5. **Should Statements**: Constantly telling yourself how things "should" or "must" be, leading to guilt or frustration.

By spotting these distortions, you can challenge them. For example, if you catch yourself catastrophizing, ask, "Is it really the worst thing that can happen, or am I jumping to extremes?" This mental check can help you see a more balanced view.

Why We Resist Changing Our Thoughts

You might wonder why we keep repeating harmful thought patterns if they cause so much trouble. One reason is that change requires effort and feels uncertain. Overthinking might be uncomfortable, but it is also familiar. The mind likes routines, even if they are negative. Breaking an old pattern means stepping into something new, which can feel scary.

Another reason is that some people believe overthinking keeps them safe. They might think, "If I worry about every possible outcome, I'll never be caught off guard." But this is not true. Overthinking can paralyze you from taking real action, and it drains your energy. Being prepared is different from being stuck in endless worry.

The Mind-Body Connection

We cannot forget that our thoughts do not only affect our feelings; they also affect our bodies. Persistent overthinking can lead to:

- **Muscle Tension**: Neck, shoulders, and back pain can all come from stress held in the body.
- **Digestive Problems**: Anxiety can disrupt digestion, causing issues like acid reflux or stomach cramps.
- **Insomnia**: Racing thoughts keep you awake at night.
- **Frequent Illness**: High stress levels can weaken the immune system, making you more prone to colds and other illnesses.

Conversely, taking care of your body—through exercise, proper sleep, and balanced nutrition—can help clear your mind. Physical activity releases endorphins, which improve mood, and good sleep helps your brain process and store memories without getting stuck on them.

Simple Neuroscience of Letting Go

When you consciously decide to let go of a worry, you are using your prefrontal cortex. It can send signals to the emotional parts of your brain to calm down. However, if you keep focusing on your fear, you strengthen the neural pathways that cause you to feel anxious. This is why many strategies for reducing overthinking involve shifting your focus. Techniques like focusing on your breath, counting objects in the room, or repeating a calming phrase can redirect your brain from the worried loop to a different activity. Over time, this redirection makes it easier for your brain to let go of negative thoughts.

Self-Talk and Its Influence

"Self-talk" is the inner voice that comments on everything you do. It can be helpful and motivating, or it can be harsh. If you are an overthinker, your self-talk might be filled with doubt, blame, or fear. Changing the tone of your self-talk can drastically reduce overthinking. For example, instead of saying, "I always mess up," try, "I made a mistake this time, but I can learn from it." It might feel odd at first, but regular practice can shift your mindset over time.

Embracing Curiosity Over Judgment

A helpful approach to dealing with thoughts and emotions is to become curious instead of judgmental. When a negative thought arises, rather than saying, "I hate that I'm thinking this," try saying, "Interesting. I wonder why this thought popped up." Curiosity places you in a learning mode. It allows you to step back and observe your mind without getting caught in self-blame. By doing so, you break the chain that often leads from thought to emotion to more negative thought.

Putting It All Together

1. **Know How Your Brain Works**: Realize that your mind has both logical and emotional components. Overthinking often happens when these parts misfire, causing you to focus on fears or regrets.
2. **Acknowledge the Negativity Bias**: Understand that your brain naturally gives more weight to negative thoughts. This does not mean positive things are less important; it is just how we are wired for survival.
3. **Identify Beliefs**: Notice if you hold deep-seated beliefs about yourself or the world that make you more prone to overthinking.
4. **Notice Cognitive Distortions**: Look for patterns like catastrophizing or all-or-nothing thinking. Challenge them with facts.
5. **Practice Emotional Regulation**: Use techniques such as breathing exercises, journaling, or mindfulness to manage strong emotions before they spiral into overthinking.
6. **Improve Self-Talk**: Shift from critical, fearful thoughts to more balanced, compassionate ones.

7. **Stay Curious**: Instead of judging your emotions, investigate them with kindness and an open mind.

Conclusion

Understanding the psychology behind thoughts and emotions gives you a powerful foundation for breaking the cycle of overthinking. By learning about how your brain processes information and how emotions work, you can begin to see that overthinking is not just "thinking too much"—it is a pattern shaped by beliefs, triggers, and biological responses. The good news is that with knowledge and practice, you can train your mind to let go of unhelpful loops and focus on what truly matters. In the next chapter, we will look more deeply at how overthinking shows up in day-to-day life and explore further how it can affect everything from your routine to your well-being.

Chapter 4: How Overthinking Affects Daily Life

Introduction

Overthinking does not remain just a mental exercise. It seeps into every aspect of our lives, from the moment we wake up until we go to sleep. This chapter examines how overthinking can shape our daily routines, relationships, work or school performance, and personal enjoyment. By spotting these effects, you can better understand where overthinking does the most damage and take targeted steps to reduce its hold.

The Morning Mindset

Many people begin the day with a head full of worries. Maybe you think about everything you need to accomplish, all the tasks left undone from yesterday, or mistakes you fear making. These worries can make you feel drained before you even get started. If you notice that your mind races the moment you open your eyes, it may be a sign that overthinking is controlling your day right from the start.

Simple Morning Fixes

- **Gratitude List**: Upon waking, list three things you feel thankful for. This can shift your mindset away from worry.
- **Stretch or Exercise**: Physical movement helps release tension and gets blood flowing to your brain, making it easier to manage thoughts.
- **Plan, Don't Dwell**: If you must think about the day's tasks, make a quick plan without going over the same worries too many times. Write them down and move on.

Effects on Work or School

Whether you are a student or a working adult, overthinking can turn everyday tasks into huge challenges.

1. **Procrastination**: Worrying about doing something "perfectly" can stop you from starting. A simple assignment can feel overwhelming if you imagine all the ways it could go wrong.
2. **Difficulty Making Decisions**: Work or study often requires quick choices. Overthinkers may freeze when faced with multiple options, fearing they will choose the wrong one.
3. **Reduced Productivity**: Time spent overthinking is time not spent taking action. This can lead to missed deadlines, incomplete projects, or rushed work.
4. **Imposter Syndrome**: Overthinkers often doubt their own skills, feeling like they are "faking it." They may worry constantly about being "found out," which reduces confidence and performance.

Real-Life Example

Consider a college student, Maria, who needs to write a paper. She has plenty of time, but as soon as she sits down, she thinks, "What if this topic is wrong? What if my professor hates my angle?" Instead of writing, she spends hours searching online for the "perfect approach." Before long, deadlines are near, and she must rush the paper, leading to anxiety and less polished work. Overthinking robbed her of the chance to methodically and calmly write a strong paper.

Impact on Relationships

Overthinking does not just affect you; it also impacts how you relate to people around you.

Communication Breakdowns

If you are worried about saying the wrong thing, you might either talk too much or too little. Overthinking can cause you to rehearse conversations in your head, sometimes leading to awkwardness because you are not present in the actual moment. You might misinterpret someone's tone or facial expression, assuming they are upset or disappointed in you.

Trust Issues

Overthinkers often seek hidden meanings in what others say. A simple text like, "We need to talk," might spiral into fears of being criticized or rejected. This can make you question your relationships unnecessarily. When you do finally speak to the person, you may approach the conversation with anxiety or defensiveness, creating tension where there might not have been any.

Emotional Exhaustion

Friends and family might notice you always seem "on edge" or tense. They might wonder if they did something wrong when, in truth, you are battling your own thoughts. Over time, people might step back if they feel they cannot reassure you enough or if they perceive that every interaction leads to stress. This can result in loneliness and even more overthinking.

Personal Time and Leisure

It is easy to imagine overthinking only in work or relationship contexts, but it also intrudes on personal time.

Hobbies and Interests

Overthinking can stop you from fully enjoying your hobbies. For instance, if you like painting, you might criticize every brushstroke, or if you enjoy playing a sport, you might worry too much about messing up to have fun. This perfectionist mindset drains the joy out of what should be relaxing activities.

Relaxation Difficulties

When it is time to unwind—perhaps by reading a book or watching a show—your mind might not allow you to focus. Instead, you replay arguments, mistakes, or future worries. This can make leisure time feel useless because you are not truly resting.

Social Events

Going out with friends or attending parties can trigger overthinking about how you look, what people think of you, or if you said something embarrassing. Instead of enjoying social connections, you might be stuck in your head analyzing every detail.

Physical Health Concerns

We have touched on stress hormones and the mind-body connection, but let us look more specifically at how daily life can be affected physically by overthinking.

1. **Fatigue**: Constant mental chatter tires you out. You might sleep enough hours but still wake up feeling drained.
2. **Headaches and Muscle Pain**: Tension in the shoulders, neck, or jaw is common among chronic overthinkers. The constant stress signals make muscles tight and sore.
3. **Sleep Problems**: Racing thoughts at bedtime can lead to insomnia or poor quality sleep, which in turn causes daytime drowsiness and irritability.
4. **Eating Habits**: Some people overeat when stressed, while others lose their appetite. Both extremes can harm overall health.

Financial Stress

Overthinking can extend to money matters. You may spend hours worrying about bills, potential car repairs, or future costs. While it is good to be mindful of finances, overthinking can result in a never-ending loop of "what if" scenarios that paralyze you. For instance, if you keep fearing a financial emergency, you might avoid normal expenses—like necessary car maintenance or an occasional treat. This can negatively impact your life quality and even lead to bigger problems down the road (like a car breakdown due to skipped maintenance).

Missed Opportunities

When overthinking becomes your default mode, you might pass on new opportunities out of fear. Whether it is a job promotion, a scholarship, or a trip with friends, you could talk yourself out of it by imagining all the things that could go wrong. This tendency to say "no" to avoid risk can limit personal growth and life experiences.

The Role of Regret

Ironically, missing out can lead to regret, which then fuels more overthinking. You may look back and say, "Why didn't I just go for it?" creating another loop of negative self-talk. Recognizing this pattern can push you to practice taking small, calculated risks rather than letting fear rule your decisions.

Overthinking in the Digital Age

Modern technology and social media have their benefits but can magnify overthinking in daily life.

1. **Social Media Comparison**: Seeing highlight reels of everyone's life can make you feel inadequate. You might dwell on why you are "behind" or not as successful.
2. **Constant Notifications**: Your phone or computer can interrupt you all day, making it hard to stay focused on what matters. Each notification might trigger a new cycle of thoughts.
3. **Digital Overload**: With so much information available, you might spend hours researching every question or concern you have, increasing mental clutter.

Tips for Digital Balance

- **Set Time Limits**: Decide how much time you can spend on social media or reading news.
- **Turn Off Notifications**: Especially for apps that are not crucial. This helps you remain present without constant interruptions.
- **Mindful Browsing**: When online, ask yourself, "Is this helping me, or am I spiraling into worry?"

Workplace or Classroom Environment

Overthinking can not only hurt your own performance but also affect the people around you.

- **Team Projects**: You may fear letting others down, so you overanalyze your role. This can cause stress for you and impatience for teammates who want to move forward.
- **Asking for Help**: Overthinkers might feel asking for help is a sign of weakness. They might struggle alone, missing out on tips or support.
- **Fear of Feedback**: Constructive criticism might be taken too personally, leading to sleepless nights and self-doubt.

Emotional Drain on Loved Ones

If you share a household with others, your overthinking might cause tension. You could ask for reassurance multiple times a day, worry openly about minor issues, or snap at people because you are stressed. Over time, loved ones might feel powerless to help or become irritated by the constant anxiety in the home. This can create conflicts or distance in relationships you deeply care about.

Mental Health Challenges

Persistent overthinking can be a factor in developing anxiety disorders or depression. While not everyone who overthinks will face these conditions, there is a strong connection between constantly replaying negative thoughts and experiencing ongoing anxiety or sadness.

- **Anxiety Disorders**: Overthinking fuels anxiety, creating a loop where anxiety leads to more overthinking.
- **Depression**: Continually focusing on negative aspects of life or your own perceived failings can lower mood and self-esteem.
- **Burnout**: Emotional and mental exhaustion can build up if you never allow your mind to rest.

Subtle Day-to-Day Consequences

Beyond major areas like work or relationships, overthinking pops up in small daily moments. For instance:

- **Grocery Shopping**: You may spend too long comparing products, worried about wasting money or making the "wrong choice."
- **Driving**: You might second-guess routes or driving decisions, adding tension to a routine task.
- **Household Chores**: Even simple tasks like cleaning can become overwhelming if you keep thinking about the "perfect" way to do them or worry you are not cleaning well enough.

Recognizing these small stresses can help you see how widespread overthinking is in your daily life.

Breaking the Cycle: Practical Ideas

1. **Time Blocking**
   Set aside specific time for tasks and do not let yourself go beyond that. If you are working on a report, give yourself two hours. When the time is up, move on. This forces you to act rather than keep analyzing.
2. **Task Prioritization**
   Write down the top few tasks you need to do each day. Focus on completing them first. This helps you see you are making progress, reducing the urge to dwell on everything at once.
3. **Mindful Pauses**
   A few times a day, stop and do a short mindfulness exercise—like a minute of slow breathing or focusing on your senses. This can reset your mind and lower the buildup of anxious thoughts.
4. **Talk It Out**
   If something is really bugging you, speak with a trusted friend or family member. Sometimes, simply expressing your thoughts out loud can help you see how exaggerated some worries are.
5. **Accept Imperfection**
   In daily life, aiming for "good enough" is often better than seeking perfect

results. Perfectionism usually feeds overthinking because nothing ever feels fully finished or correct.

Signs That Overthinking Has Taken Over

- **You Feel Chronically Tired**: Even with enough sleep, your mind never seems rested.
- **You Lose Interest in Activities**: Things you once enjoyed start feeling like sources of stress rather than relaxation.
- **People Close to You Comment on Your Worry**: If you frequently hear, "Don't worry so much" from multiple people, it might mean your overthinking is obvious to others.
- **You Can't Relax**: Downtime feels uncomfortable because you keep thinking about what needs to be done or what might go wrong.

The Importance of Small Wins

One way to combat overthinking in daily life is to celebrate small victories. Did you finish a chapter of a book without checking your phone every few minutes? Did you decide on a restaurant without spending an hour reading reviews? Give yourself credit. Recognizing your ability to make decisions and move forward builds confidence. That confidence can reduce the hold of overthinking over time.

Building Structure and Routine

Structure can be a strong defense against overthinking because it gives your mind a sense of certainty. If every day is unpredictable, your mind might race trying to plan for every possibility. A routine, however, reduces the number of decisions you face.

- **Morning Routine**: Wake up at the same time, eat a consistent breakfast, and do a quick meditation or journal entry.
- **Work/Study Schedule**: Block times for specific tasks and breaks.
- **Evening Wind-Down**: Turn off electronics at a set time, maybe read a book or do a calm hobby before bed.

Having these predictable elements can reduce anxiety and give you clear times to think and times to rest.

Recognizing Progress

It is important to keep track of improvements, no matter how small. Overthinkers sometimes set very high expectations. If you are used to overthinking for hours, and you cut it down to 30 minutes, that is progress worth noting. You might keep a simple log: "Today I worried about X for 15 minutes, then shifted to a new activity." Over time, you will see trends and realize you can handle worries without dwelling on them endlessly.

Long-Term Effects If Left Unchecked

If overthinking continues without any attempt to manage or reduce it, you could face:

- **Chronic Stress-Related Illness**: High blood pressure, heart disease, or frequent migraines.
- **Social Isolation**: If friends and family feel that every interaction is heavy, they might distance themselves.
- **Lack of Self-Esteem**: Constant self-doubt can erode your sense of worth, making you feel powerless.
- **Missed Life Experiences**: You may look back with regret on things you avoided due to fear.

Recognizing these potential outcomes can serve as motivation to address overthinking now rather than waiting.

Conclusion

Overthinking affects almost every corner of daily life, from the moment we wake up until we close our eyes at night. It can turn simple tasks into big worries, strain relationships, harm work or school performance, and even lead to physical health problems. The good news is that by paying attention to how overthinking shows up in your routine, you can begin to make small yet meaningful changes.

These changes add up, helping you find more peace, clarity, and genuine enjoyment in your everyday activities.

As we move on to the next chapters, we will build on this knowledge to create practical strategies for breaking free from overthinking. We will cover awareness, thought-pattern creation, and a range of techniques to quiet the mind. The more you understand exactly how and where overthinking creeps in, the easier it becomes to push it out and live in a calmer, more focused state. Keep in mind that progress takes time. Each small step you take will bring you closer to a life less burdened by racing thoughts and more guided by clarity and purpose.

Chapter 5: Building Awareness: Recognizing Your Triggers

Introduction

Overthinking does not happen out of nowhere. It starts with a trigger—something that sparks a chain of thoughts and emotions. You might notice a sudden worry, a memory, or a fear of an upcoming event, and before you know it, you are stuck in mental loops. In previous chapters, we touched on what triggers are and how they lead to overthinking. This chapter will go deeper, helping you systematically identify and understand these triggers. By learning practical steps to become more aware, you can catch overthinking sooner and manage it better.

Building awareness is like turning on a light in a dark room. Once you see what is there, you can work around it instead of stumbling. We will explore why awareness matters, how to spot your unique overthinking patterns, and what methods can help you manage triggers more effectively.

---

1. Why Awareness Matters

Awareness is the first step in breaking any cycle. Imagine you want to fix a leaky faucet. If you do not notice the drip, you cannot take action. In the same way, if you never realize that certain topics or situations set off your overthinking, you remain stuck. Awareness gives you the power to see the early warning signs, so you do not have to be controlled by racing thoughts.

The Early Catch

When you notice a trigger early, you have more tools at your disposal to handle it. You might choose a breathing exercise, distract yourself with a task, or talk to someone you trust. If you do not notice the trigger, you might let your thoughts build up until it is much harder to calm down.

Preventing Escalation

By recognizing triggers quickly, you can prevent small worries from escalating into huge anxieties. Instead of letting one negative comment spin into hours of self-doubt, you can step in and challenge that thought pattern before it gains momentum. This can save you a great deal of stress and mental exhaustion.

---

2. Understanding Internal vs. External Triggers

Triggers can be internal or external. Some come from your surroundings (external), and others come from within (internal). Knowing the difference helps you pinpoint what kind of changes you might need to make.

External Triggers

External triggers include situations or events in the world around you. Examples are:

- A tense conversation with a coworker
- Receiving a critical message from your boss or teacher
- Unexpected bills or financial concerns
- Traffic jams or crowded public spaces
- Social events where you feel judged

These outside conditions can spark worry. While you cannot always control external triggers (like traffic or weather), you can control how you respond to them.

Internal Triggers

Internal triggers start within you. They can be:

- Certain memories, like recalling an embarrassing moment
- Anxious physical sensations, such as a racing heart or jittery feeling
- Self-doubt or recurring negative thoughts about your abilities
- Personal beliefs that get activated when you face potential failure

Because internal triggers lie inside the mind, you might not immediately notice them. You may have a random thought that says, "I'm not good enough," and suddenly you find yourself in a worry spiral. Recognizing these internal cues is crucial to stopping overthinking before it ramps up.

---

3. Mapping Out Your Typical Triggers

Everyone's triggers are different. Some people get anxious about social events, while others are more concerned about health or money. One way to start seeing patterns is to create a "trigger map."

How to Create a Trigger Map

1. **Notebook or Digital Document**: Find a consistent place to record your thoughts.
2. **Write Down the Situation**: Whenever you catch yourself overthinking, note the time, place, and what was happening.
3. **Identify the Trigger**: Was it a conversation, a thought, a physical sensation?
4. **Record Your Emotional Reaction**: How did you feel right after the trigger? Fearful, angry, sad?
5. **Note Your Thoughts**: Write the main worries that appeared.

By reviewing these notes regularly, you can see common patterns. Maybe most of your overthinking episodes happen after checking social media or during quiet times before bed. Once you know these patterns, you can prepare or adjust your habits.

Frequency and Intensity

Also note how often a certain trigger affects you and how intense your reaction is. For example, a conflict with a friend might cause mild anxiety, but a conversation with your boss might cause full-blown panic. Knowing which triggers are "bigger" can help you decide where to focus your coping strategies first.

4. Body and Mind Signals

In the previous chapter, we touched on how overthinking affects daily life. Here, we will talk about how your body and mind give signals when a trigger occurs. Recognizing these signals is key to catching overthinking early.

Physical Signs

- **Tense Muscles**: Shoulders hunch up, jaw feels tight.
- **Stomach Discomfort**: Nausea, knots in your stomach, or a sudden drop in appetite.
- **Fast Heart Rate**: Feeling your heart pounding.
- **Sweaty Palms**: Hands become clammy.
- **Quick, Shallow Breathing**: You might even feel lightheaded if you are very anxious.

Emotional Signs

- **Sudden Drop in Mood**: Feeling sad or hopeless quickly.
- **Rising Irritability**: Getting annoyed at small things.
- **Strong Urge to Escape**: Wanting to leave the situation right away.
- **Nervous Energy**: Feeling like you cannot sit still, tapping your foot or fidgeting.

When you notice these signs, pause and ask, "What might have caused this sudden change?" Often, you will find a trigger occurred—maybe you read an upsetting email or had an unsettling thought. By becoming sensitive to these signals, you build awareness that leads to better handling of your triggers.

5. Differentiating Reality From Assumption

Sometimes, a big part of recognizing triggers involves sorting out what is real from what you assume. For example, if you get a short text from a friend that says "We need to talk," you might assume something bad has happened. Yet, the actual reality might be that your friend is planning a surprise party and needs your help.

The Story vs. The Fact

- **Fact**: Your friend wants to talk.
- **Story**: You imagine they are angry or upset with you.

Overthinking often happens because our mind creates stories around facts. By separating the two, you can see if a trigger is truly a concern or just a misunderstanding.

Check for Evidence

When you feel triggered, ask yourself:

- "Do I have proof that something bad has happened?"
- "Is there an alternative explanation?"
- "Am I jumping to conclusions?"

This quick mental check can help you stop overthinking triggered by assumptions, reducing unnecessary stress.

---

6. Triggers Tied to Past Trauma or Painful Events

Some triggers are rooted in deeper emotional wounds. If you experienced bullying, a serious accident, or a difficult breakup, you might respond strongly to anything that reminds you of that event. This kind of trigger can be more complex because it taps into unresolved pain.

Recognizing Trauma-Linked Triggers

- They often produce very strong emotional reactions, sometimes out of proportion to the current event.
- They might bring flashbacks or vivid memories.
- Physical reactions can be intense—like shaking, crying, or feeling frozen.

If you suspect a trigger is tied to a past trauma, it might be worth seeking professional help. A counselor or therapist can guide you in processing these experiences so they lose their strong hold over your present. Becoming aware of these triggers is the first step toward healing and reducing overthinking tied to your past.

---

7. Practical Techniques to Increase Awareness

Sometimes, it is hard to notice triggers because we move through life on autopilot. Fortunately, you can train yourself to become more mindful.

7.1 Mindful Check-Ins

Set an alarm on your phone or watch, maybe once every few hours. When it goes off, pause for 30 seconds. Ask yourself:

- "What am I feeling right now?"
- "Have I been worrying or overthinking anything?"
- "What triggered these thoughts or feelings?"

This small pause helps break automatic patterns. You might discover you were ruminating about a conversation from earlier in the day without consciously realizing it.

7.2 Body Scan

A body scan is a simple exercise to tune in to physical sensations:

1. Sit or lie down comfortably.
2. Close your eyes and take a deep breath.
3. Start from the top of your head and mentally move down to your toes.
4. At each part (forehead, jaw, neck, shoulders, etc.), notice if it is tense or relaxed.
5. If you find tension, gently try to release it.

By regularly doing a body scan, you become more attuned to the physical signals that often accompany an overthinking trigger. If your shoulders suddenly tense up during the day, you can pause and figure out what thought or event caused it.

7.3 Trigger Journaling

We mentioned the idea of a trigger map. To expand on this, consider keeping a daily or weekly trigger journal. It does not need to be long—just a quick note of each time you notice yourself entering a worry spiral. Over time, patterns will emerge. You might find certain times of day or specific situations always spark overthinking. This knowledge is invaluable for planning how to handle or avoid triggers in the future.

7.4 Sharing With a Friend or Mentor

If you find it difficult to identify triggers alone, consider talking to someone you trust about your experiences. They might notice patterns you overlook. For instance, a close friend might point out that you always seem anxious after scrolling through social media at night. Hearing an outside perspective can illuminate blind spots.

---

8. Adjusting Your Environment to Reduce Triggers

Awareness is not just about noticing triggers; it can also guide you to make changes to your environment or routines to reduce unnecessary stress.

8.1 Decluttering Your Spaces

A messy or disorganized area can add low-level stress that makes you more prone to overthinking. If possible, keep your home or work area tidy. For example, if you always see piles of unopened mail, you might feel anxious about finances, fueling overthinking. Sorting or organizing it regularly can remove that trigger.

8.2 Setting Boundaries

If certain people or situations repeatedly trigger you, consider setting boundaries. This might mean limiting time with a negative friend, adjusting your social media usage, or asking for clearer communication from coworkers. While you cannot avoid all triggers, you can reduce the ones that are predictable and unhelpful.

8.3 Healthy Lifestyle Habits

We often forget that basic habits like sleep, diet, and exercise can affect how sensitive we are to triggers. When you are well-rested, you handle stress more calmly. If you are tired or running on caffeine and sugar, you might get triggered more easily. Think of a balanced lifestyle as a buffer that helps you stay grounded, so triggers do not knock you off balance as much.

---

9. Creating a Trigger Action Plan

Now that we have explored various ways to become more aware of triggers, the next step is turning that knowledge into action. A Trigger Action Plan is a simple set of steps you can follow when you notice overthinking starting up.

9.1 Step One: Acknowledge the Trigger

Say to yourself, "I'm feeling anxious because I just saw that email," or "My shoulders tensed up when I remembered last week's mistake." Naming the trigger reduces its power by bringing it into the open.

9.2 Step Two: Take a Calming Action

Pick one simple action to help you calm down:

- Take three deep breaths, inhaling for four seconds, holding for four, and exhaling for four.
- Step away from your phone or desk and do a quick walk around the block.
- Listen to a soothing song for a minute.

This helps break the immediate rush of anxiety or stress.

9.3 Step Three: Reframe or Question the Thought

Ask yourself:

- "Is there another way to see this?"
- "What advice would I give a friend in this situation?"
- "Am I magnifying this problem beyond what it deserves?"

Sometimes, just challenging your first reaction helps you see the situation more clearly.

9.4 Step Four: Decide on Next Steps

Finally, decide if you need to do anything about the trigger. Sometimes, you can let it go. Other times, you might need to clarify something with a person involved. Choose one small, concrete action if necessary (e.g., "I will email my boss for details instead of assuming the worst"). Following this plan consistently helps train your mind to respond in healthier ways.

---

10. Conclusion

Building awareness is like learning to read your own mind's weather report. By recognizing triggers early, observing how your body and mind react, and keeping track of patterns, you gain the power to stop overthinking before it becomes overwhelming. This chapter focused on becoming more alert to what sets your thoughts in motion and how to respond productively. You now have a toolbox that includes mindful check-ins, body scans, trigger journaling, and environmental adjustments.

Remember that awareness is not about avoiding every challenge. Triggers will happen. But with awareness, you can face them from a place of calm understanding instead of panic or confusion. Over time, this practice will make you more resilient and less vulnerable to spiraling thoughts.

Chapter 6: Creating Helpful Thought Patterns

Introduction

Now that you understand how to recognize and manage your triggers, the next stage involves shaping your thoughts so they support rather than sabotage you. Overthinking often involves repetitive and negative thought loops. If we want to quiet the mind, we need to replace these loops with healthier, more balanced patterns. This chapter explores techniques for challenging negative thoughts and creating new, helpful ways of thinking. By applying these methods, you take an active role in guiding your mind, rather than letting it run on autopilot.

---

1. What Are Thought Patterns?

A "thought pattern" is like a path your mind follows when interpreting events. Some patterns are helpful, encouraging you to see challenges as solvable. Others are harmful, trapping you in self-doubt or worry. Picture a well-worn trail in the forest—the more you walk it, the more permanent it becomes. In the same way, the more you think a certain way, the stronger that thought pattern becomes.

Why Thought Patterns Matter

1. **Emotional Well-Being**: Your patterns shape how you feel day to day. Negative loops produce anxiety, sadness, or anger, while positive loops lead to calmness or optimism.
2. **Decision-Making**: If your pattern is "I will fail anyway," you might avoid trying new things. If your pattern is "I can learn from mistakes," you are more likely to take healthy risks.
3. **Self-Esteem**: Harmful patterns can damage how you see yourself, making you feel less capable. Positive patterns build self-confidence and resilience.

2. Identifying Negative Thought Patterns

Before you can change something, you need to see it clearly. Identifying negative patterns is the next logical step after becoming aware of your triggers. Common examples include:

1. **Catastrophizing**: Always expecting the worst-case scenario.
2. **Black-and-White Thinking**: Believing events or people are all good or all bad, with no middle ground.
3. **Mind Reading**: Assuming you know what others are thinking, often in a negative way ("They must think I'm incompetent").
4. **Personalization**: Taking events too personally, even if they have little to do with you.
5. **Should Statements**: Telling yourself things "should" be a certain way, leading to disappointment or anger when reality differs.

Ask yourself which of these ring true. You might recognize several or just one. The key is to spot them when they pop up so you can start to shift them.

---

3. Challenging Your Thoughts: The "Why?" Method

A useful method for tackling negative thoughts is simply asking "why?" multiple times. This helps peel away layers to reach the core issue.

1. **Start With the Thought**: "I'm sure I'll mess up my presentation."
2. **Ask 'Why?'**: "Why do I think I'll mess up?" Maybe because you are afraid you will forget your lines.
3. **Ask 'Why?' Again**: "Why am I afraid I'll forget my lines?" Perhaps you recall a past embarrassment in front of people.
4. **Keep Going**: The deeper you go, the more you see that the real fear might be of public shame or rejection, rather than just forgetting a line.

Once you identify the core fear, you can address it. Maybe you decide to practice more or prepare note cards. Or you remind yourself that one past event does not guarantee the future. This "Why?" method shows you that your negative thought might be based on old worries rather than current reality.

4. Thought Replacement: Swapping Negative for Positive

Sometimes, it helps to create a direct alternative statement for each negative thought. This is called "thought replacement."

Steps to Practice Thought Replacement

1. **Spot the Negative Thought**: e.g., "I'll never be good at this job."
2. **Acknowledge It**: Mentally say, "I notice this negative belief."
3. **Write a Balanced Alternative**: e.g., "I'm learning every day, and I can improve with practice."
4. **Repeat and Reinforce**: Each time the negative thought resurfaces, consciously replace it with the balanced one.

Notice we used the word "balanced." We do not want to move from "I'll never be good at this job" to something unrealistic like "I'm the best in the world, and I can't fail." A realistic, constructive statement is more likely to stick in your mind.

Example in Action

- **Old Thought**: "I'm a terrible student."
- **New Thought**: "I have struggled with some subjects, but I can do better by studying consistently and asking for help."

With repetition, your brain forms a new path. It might feel forced at first, but over time, the new thought gains strength.

---

5. Using Affirmations Properly

Affirmations are short, positive statements you repeat to yourself. They can be powerful if used correctly, but they should feel believable. Telling yourself, "I'm perfect in every way" might feel false and do more harm than good. Instead, pick affirmations that acknowledge reality but still uplift you.

Crafting Genuine Affirmations

- Use "I can" or "I am learning" statements: "I am learning to handle challenges calmly."
- Focus on small steps: "I am improving a bit more each day."
- Keep them specific: "I am capable of speaking confidently in team meetings."

Repeat these affirmations daily—while looking in the mirror, during a short walk, or before you go to bed. Over time, they become part of your usual thought pattern.

---

6. The Power of Questions in Forming New Thoughts

Questions can reshape your thinking, sometimes more effectively than statements. For instance, if you catch yourself saying, "I can't do this," try asking, "How can I make this doable?" A question engages your brain in finding solutions rather than shutting down.

Examples of Helpful Questions

- "What is one small step I can take to start?"
- "Who can I ask for guidance?"
- "Have I faced something similar before and succeeded?"
- "Is there another way to look at this problem?"

These questions push your mind to be proactive. It shifts your focus from worrying to problem-solving.

---

7. Thought-Stopping Techniques

Sometimes, a negative loop is so intense, you need a quick method to interrupt it right away. Thought-stopping can be a short-term fix to break free from spiraling thoughts.

7.1 Visual or Verbal Cue

You might imagine a stop sign in your head or say "Stop!" out loud (if you are alone). This sudden cue can jolt you out of a negative thought loop. Right after this, replace the thought with something more balanced or direct your attention to another task.

7.2 Physical Movement

When you are stuck in your head, do something physical for a few minutes:

- Jumping jacks
- Stretching
- Shaking out your arms
- Taking a brief walk

The burst of movement can disrupt overthinking patterns. It also reminds you that you are in control of your body and mind.

7.3 Grounding Yourself in the Present

Grounding techniques bring you back to the "now." You might:

- Describe your surroundings: "I see a blue wall, a brown desk, and a red carpet."
- Touch something nearby and note its texture.
- Focus on deep, slow breathing, noticing how it feels.

This helps shift your attention away from future worries or past regrets, anchoring you to the present moment.

8. Encouraging Flexible Thinking

Many harmful thought patterns are rigid. They say, "It must be this way," or "It has to be that way." Flexible thinking allows for multiple possibilities. Instead of seeing a problem as either a success or a failure, you see shades of grey and room for growth.

Methods to Boost Flexibility

1. **Brainstorm Outcomes**: When worried, list all possible outcomes—from best to worst. Often, you will find many in-between scenarios.
2. **Try New Activities**: Learning something fresh, like a language or hobby, teaches your brain to adapt. This sense of adaptability can carry over into your thinking.
3. **Seek Diverse Opinions**: Talk to people with different backgrounds or viewpoints. Hearing varied perspectives trains your mind to be open and less likely to cling to one negative narrative.

---

9. Practical Exercises to Strengthen Helpful Thoughts

9.1 The "Evidence For and Against" Chart

Make two columns on a piece of paper: "Evidence For" and "Evidence Against." Suppose your worry is "I'm going to fail this test." Under "Evidence For," maybe you write, "I struggled with the last quiz." Under "Evidence Against," perhaps you list, "I studied more this time, I did fine on homework, my teacher said I showed improvement." Seeing the balanced picture can help you feel calmer and more prepared.

9.2 Journaling for Self-Reflection

Writing down your day and how you reacted to events can reveal patterns in your thinking. Ask yourself:

- "Which thoughts helped me today?"
- "Which thoughts hurt my mood or performance?"
- "How can I reframe the hurtful thoughts?"

By committing this to paper (or a digital journal), you make the process of changing thought patterns more concrete.

9.3 Role Reversal

If you are judging yourself harshly, imagine a friend telling you the same story about themselves. What would you say to comfort or advise them? By playing the role of adviser, you might generate kinder, more supportive thoughts, realizing you deserve that same compassion.

---

10. Maintaining New Thought Patterns

Learning to create helpful thoughts is not a quick fix. It is more like training for a marathon: you improve with consistency over time. Once you start seeing benefits, the challenge is to maintain these new habits.

Overcoming Setbacks

Expect setbacks. You might find yourself reverting to old thoughts during high stress. That is normal. The key is noticing when you slip up and getting back on track without beating yourself up. Each setback can be a chance to learn. Ask, "What triggered me?" and "How can I handle it next time?"

Rewarding Your Progress

It can be motivating to reward yourself for small wins. If you catch a negative thought and replace it, give yourself a mental pat on the back. Maybe treat yourself to a relaxing bath or an episode of a favorite show. Positive reinforcement keeps you engaged in the process.

Pairing Up With Accountability

Sometimes it helps to have a friend or family member you check in with. If you are both working on healthier thinking, you can support each other. Or you can simply share your goals and let them know you might appreciate a gentle reminder if they see you spiraling into negative thoughts.

---

11. Real-Life Example: James' Journey

James was a college student who constantly worried about social acceptance. If a classmate did not say hello, James thought, "They hate me now." Recognizing this was a negative assumption, he started using "thought replacement." Each time he caught himself believing someone disliked him with no evidence, he replaced it with: "Maybe they were busy or didn't see me."

Over time, James noticed he felt less anxious walking around campus. He also tried flexible thinking, reminding himself that even if one person was upset, he had other friends who supported him. This shift in thought patterns took a few months, but by the end of the semester, James reported feeling much calmer and more confident in social settings.

---

12. Tying It All Together

You have spent the previous chapter learning to recognize triggers (Chapter 5). Now, you know that once those triggers appear, the next step is to shape your thought patterns intentionally. You can use a variety of techniques—thought replacement, affirmations, grounding, and flexible thinking—to stop negative loops.

Here is a simple flow you might use:

1. **Trigger Occurs**: You notice stress or a negative thought.
2. **Pause and Breathe**: Take a mindful moment to center yourself.

3. **Challenge the Thought**: Use "Why?" or the "Evidence For and Against" chart to see if your worry is realistic.
4. **Replace or Reframe**: Swap the negative thought for a balanced perspective.
5. **Continue With Your Activity**: Return to your day with a calmer mindset.

With practice, this becomes more natural. Eventually, you might catch yourself changing your thoughts without consciously going through every step, because you have rewired your mental habits.

---

13. Conclusion

Creating helpful thought patterns is a powerful way to quiet an overactive mind. Instead of letting triggers launch you into the same anxious loops, you can respond with a calmer, solution-focused approach. Thought replacement, affirmations, and grounding techniques are just some of the tools to help you reshape how you think—and how you feel.

Remember: this process takes time and patience. You are effectively teaching your brain new habits, just as you would teach a child how to tie their shoes. The more you practice, the more automatic these positive patterns become. Eventually, overthinking loses its grip, and you gain mental space for creativity, problem-solving, and joy.

In the chapters to come, we will continue to explore strategies to help you manage your emotions, build routines for clarity, and strengthen your mind and body to handle life's challenges without sinking into worry. Each new tool will reinforce what you have learned so far, guiding you toward a future where overthinking plays a smaller, more manageable role.

Chapter 7: Techniques to Quiet the Mind

Introduction

In the last chapters, we discussed how to recognize triggers and create healthier thought patterns. Now, let us focus on specific techniques you can use to calm your mind. When you notice the first signs of overthinking—racing thoughts, tightening muscles, or worry about future scenarios—you can apply these methods to regain clarity and composure. Think of them as a toolkit from which you can pick what works best for you at different moments.

Over time, practicing these techniques can help you form a habit of tranquility. You will get better at spotting overthinking in its early stages and stopping it from spiraling. Even if you already know a few calming approaches, this chapter aims to deepen your understanding and offer new ideas so you can create a well-rounded routine that supports a quieter mind.

---

1. The Power of Stillness

A busy mind often craves constant activity. We fill each moment with noise—social media, tasks, background music, or constant thoughts about what is next. In this state, the brain rarely has a chance to rest. One of the simplest yet most overlooked techniques is stillness: intentionally slowing down and sitting quietly, even if for only a few minutes.

Benefits of Embracing Stillness

- **Mental Reset**: Pausing your usual rush of thoughts gives your mind a chance to breathe.
- **Heightened Awareness**: You become more alert to small details, such as your breathing or the sounds around you.

- **Lower Stress Levels**: Stillness helps the body reduce stress hormones, easing muscle tension and lowering heart rate.

How to Practice Stillness

1. **Choose a Quiet Place**: Find a spot in your home or outdoors where you feel safe and calm.
2. **Set a Timer**: Start with just two to three minutes, slowly extending to five or ten as you grow comfortable.
3. **Sit Comfortably**: You can sit on a chair or on the floor, making sure your back is supported.
4. **Do Nothing**: Resist the urge to check your phone, read, or even plan your day. Your only "task" is to let your mind settle.
5. **Notice What Arises**: If thoughts come, acknowledge them without judgment and let them pass. Return to the calm of simply being there.

At first, it may feel odd or even uncomfortable to sit still. However, with regular practice, you might find it surprisingly refreshing. Over time, these short moments of quiet can anchor you when life gets hectic.

---

2. Mindfulness Meditation

Mindfulness is about paying full attention to the present moment without judgment. When you practice mindfulness meditation, you focus on something like your breath or your senses, gently returning your attention whenever your thoughts wander.

Basic Steps

1. **Pick a Posture**: You can sit on a cushion, chair, or even lie down if you prefer—just remain relaxed but alert.
2. **Settle the Body**: Take a few deep breaths, noticing how it feels. Close your eyes if that helps you focus.
3. **Breath as an Anchor**: Pay attention to each inhale and exhale. Where do you feel the breath most—your nose, chest, or belly?

4. **Observe Thoughts**: If you notice your mind drifting to planning dinner or replaying a mistake, quietly bring your focus back to the breath.
5. **No Judgment**: It is natural to have thoughts. The goal is not to have a blank mind but to gently guide yourself back each time you wander.

Mindfulness in Everyday Life

Mindfulness does not have to be limited to formal meditation. You can do daily tasks—like washing dishes, brushing your teeth, or walking the dog—mindfully by fully focusing on each action rather than letting your mind roam. This helps train the habit of staying present, reducing overthinking about the past or future.

---

3. Deep Breathing and Progressive Muscle Relaxation

When you start to overthink, your body often responds with tension: shallow breathing, a racing heart, tight shoulders. By shifting how you breathe, you can quickly reduce these physical signs of stress. Progressive muscle relaxation adds another layer, helping you systematically release tension.

Deep Breathing Technique

1. **Find a Comfortable Position**: Sit or lie down, placing one hand on your chest and the other on your belly.
2. **Inhale Slowly**: Breathe in through your nose for a count of four. Feel your belly rise as air fills that area.
3. **Pause**: Hold your breath for a brief moment (about one or two seconds).
4. **Exhale Gently**: Breathe out through your mouth for a count of four. Notice your belly falling.
5. **Repeat**: Continue for several cycles. Focus on making each breath steady and slow.

Progressive Muscle Relaxation

1. **Tense a Muscle Group**: Start with your feet. Curl your toes and tense the muscles for a few seconds.
2. **Relax**: Release the tension and let your foot muscles go limp, noticing the contrast between tense and relaxed.
3. **Move Up the Body**: Next, tense your calves, then your thighs, moving gradually to your hands, arms, shoulders, and face.
4. **Maintain Steady Breathing**: While doing this, keep breathing deeply to further enhance relaxation.

Both methods help you become aware of tension and practice letting it go—an essential skill for quieting the mind when overthinking kicks in.

---

4. "Worry Box" or "Worry Time" Technique

Sometimes, trying to force yourself not to worry only makes the worries stronger. Instead, you can schedule a brief period each day to concentrate on your concerns, placing them in a mental "worry box" for that designated time.

Steps for the Worry Box

1. **Choose a Specific Time**: Perhaps 15 minutes each evening.
2. **Write or Think Freely**: During that slot, list your worries without holding back. Do not try to solve them yet; just get them out.
3. **Stop After Time Is Up**: Once the worry time ends, close your notepad or mentally "lock" the worry box. Remind yourself to wait until the next scheduled session before dwelling on them again.
4. **Freedom Outside Worry Time**: If a worry pops up at another time, gently say, "Not now; I'll handle you later."

This method trains your mind to recognize that worries have their place, but they do not get to control the rest of your day. You might find that when "worry time" arrives, some concerns already seem less important, showing you how overthinking can diminish when not constantly fed.

5. Journaling Approaches

Writing is a powerful way to release thoughts from your head onto paper. Several journaling styles can help you quiet your mind:

5.1 Free-Writing (Stream of Consciousness)

Set a timer for 10 to 15 minutes. Write down everything that comes to mind, without editing or worrying about punctuation. Let the words flow. This type of journaling often reveals hidden worries or patterns of thought you did not notice before.

5.2 Prompt-Based Journaling

Use a question to guide your writing. For example:

- "What is the main thing on my mind today?"
- "What can I control, and what is beyond my control?"
- "How can I be kinder to myself right now?"

Answering prompts helps you focus on solutions or insights rather than just venting.

5.3 Gratitude Journaling

End or begin the day by listing three things you are grateful for. They can be small—like a good cup of coffee, a pleasant conversation, or your favorite cozy blanket. Gratitude shifts your attention away from worries, reminding you of positives in your life. This can create a calmer mind-state over time.

---

6. Visualization Techniques

Visualization uses the imagination to guide your thoughts toward calmer, happier places. This can be especially helpful if you tend to picture negative or scary outcomes. By consciously visualizing something soothing or positive, you redirect mental energy and settle your nerves.

Peaceful Place Visualization

1. **Close Your Eyes**: Sit comfortably and breathe slowly.
2. **Imagine a Calming Scene**: It could be a beach, a forest, a favorite room—anywhere you feel safe and relaxed.
3. **Use Your Senses**: Hear the waves, smell the pine trees, feel the sun's warmth, or taste a refreshing breeze. The more senses you involve, the more real the scene feels.
4. **Stay a While**: Spend a few minutes enjoying this mental place. Notice your body relaxing.
5. **Return Gently**: When ready, open your eyes. Carry a bit of that peace back with you to the present moment.

Positive Outcome Visualization

If you are nervous about a specific event—like a test or a meeting—visualize yourself successfully handling it. See yourself calm, confident, and performing well. This approach helps replace worst-case scenario thinking with a more balanced, optimistic image.

---

7. Physical Movement and Yoga

While quiet practices like meditation and journaling are great for calming the mind, sometimes movement is the key. Exercise releases endorphins, which naturally lift your mood and reduce stress. Yoga, in particular, combines movement with mindful focus on breathing and posture.

Gentle Movement for a Busy Mind

- **Walking**: Even a short, mindful walk can clear away mental clutter. Focus on your footsteps, the air on your skin, or the rhythm of your breath.
- **Light Stretching**: Simple stretches in the morning or before bed help relieve tension built up in your body. As your muscles loosen, your mind often relaxes as well.
- **Dancing**: Put on music you enjoy and move freely. Dancing is an expressive release that can shift your emotional state quickly.

Yoga Basics

- **Child's Pose**: A gentle pose that helps you slow your breath and stretch your lower back.
- **Cat-Cow Stretch**: Good for releasing tension in the spine and getting in tune with rhythmic breathing.
- **Sun Salutation**: A sequence of poses that warms up the entire body.

You do not have to be flexible or advanced in yoga. Start with simple poses. The key is combining movement with intentional breathing, anchoring your mind to the present.

---

8. Digital Detox and Screen Breaks

In modern life, screens are everywhere. They keep us connected but can also lead to mental overload—constant notifications, news cycles, social comparisons, and more. Taking short breaks from devices can significantly help in quieting the mind.

Planning a Digital Detox

1. **Set Time Limits**: Decide on periods where you will not check any devices—maybe after 8 p.m. or during the first hour of your morning.
2. **Turn Off Non-Essential Notifications**: Check apps on your own schedule rather than being interrupted by alerts.
3. **Create Device-Free Zones**: Keep your bedroom or dining table free of phones and laptops. This preserves those areas for rest and connection.
4. **Fill the Space**: If you suddenly have free moments without a phone in your hand, use them to reflect, breathe, or engage in a hobby.

By reducing digital noise, you allow your mind more room to process thoughts calmly, instead of reacting to a never-ending stream of information.

9. Creative Expression as a Calming Tool

Overthinking often involves words and ideas swirling inside the mind. Creative outlets give these internal energies a new shape. Whether you are artistic or not, the act of creating something can anchor you in the moment and soothe an anxious mind.

Forms of Creative Expression

- **Drawing or Painting**: You do not need to be a skilled artist. Even doodling can relieve tension.
- **Playing Music or Singing**: Music has a powerful emotional effect. Singing can also help regulate your breathing.
- **Crafting**: Knitting, scrapbooking, pottery—hands-on tasks that require focus can shift your mind from worry to creation.
- **Writing Poetry or Short Stories**: Channel your busy thoughts into a creative piece. It can help you transform worries into art, giving them a new perspective.

---

10. Putting It All Together: Making a Personal Plan

Having multiple techniques is great, but implementing them in daily life works best when you have a plan. Overthinking does not always politely wait for free time—it can hit at random. Here is a simple approach to weaving these methods into your routine:

1. **Morning Ritual**
    - Upon waking, take a couple of minutes of stillness or do a short breathing exercise.
    - If you have time, jot down a quick gratitude list or do a gentle stretch.
2. **Midday Check-In**
    - During lunch or a short break, try a quick mindful breathing session.
    - If worries about work or school pop up, jot them down in a worry journal so they do not run wild in your head.

3. **Evening Wind-Down**
    - Set aside "worry time" if you have lingering concerns.
    - Practice a 5- or 10-minute mindfulness meditation or do some light yoga to release tension from the day.
    - Avoid heavy screen use just before bed, letting your mind relax naturally.
4. **Emergency Tools**
    - If a sudden wave of overthinking hits, use a rapid "Stop!" cue, do a brief grounding exercise, or take a short walk.
    - Keep a small notebook or app where you can quickly write or record anxious thoughts, then return to them later if needed.

Over time, these daily habits can help you maintain a calmer baseline. When overthinking flares up, you are already equipped to deal with it swiftly and effectively.

---

11. Maintaining Consistency

It is common to start strong with new techniques, then slip back into old habits during busy or stressful periods. The key is consistency. Even small daily doses of mindfulness or breathing exercises can build resilience. If you miss a day or feel like you "failed," remember this process is not about perfection—it is about returning to the tools that help you whenever you notice yourself drifting.

Celebrate Small Wins

Got through a stressful meeting without spiraling into panic? That is progress. Did you take two minutes of deep breathing before bed? That is also progress. Acknowledging small successes encourages you to keep going, forming a positive cycle.

12. Conclusion

Quieting the mind is not about eliminating all thoughts—an impossible task—but about guiding your mental energy toward healthier, calmer states. The techniques in this chapter, from stillness and mindfulness meditation to journaling and yoga, are practical ways to steer your thoughts when overthinking arises. You do not have to try all of them at once. Experiment to see which methods suit your life and personality best.

Over time, as you practice these approaches, you may notice you bounce back more quickly from stress and that your periods of peace grow longer. This is part of training your mind to remain steady in the face of triggers or challenges. In the next chapter, we will build on this skill set by focusing on **developing emotional resilience**—the ability to handle life's ups and downs without getting stuck in worry or fear. Together, these tools will help you create a lasting foundation for a calmer, more balanced life.

Chapter 8: Developing Emotional Resilience

Introduction

Life can be unpredictable. At times, you might face challenges such as job changes, family conflicts, or personal disappointments that test your mental strength. Emotional resilience is what helps you weather these storms without collapsing into overthinking or despair. It is the ability to bounce back from difficult events and adapt to new realities. Building emotional resilience is not about becoming cold or never feeling sadness—rather, it is about learning to handle emotions in a healthy way and recovering more quickly when you feel overwhelmed.

In this chapter, we will explore practical steps to strengthen your resilience, allowing you to navigate life's hurdles while keeping your mind clear and focused. We will look at the components of resilience, ways to handle setbacks, and how to maintain a steady mindset even when facing uncertainty.

---

1. What Is Emotional Resilience?

Think of resilience like a rubber band. When stretched, a rubber band can bend quite far, but it snaps back to its original shape when the tension releases. Emotional resilience acts in a similar way for your mind and emotions. Rather than breaking when life pulls you in tough directions, you adapt and return to a stable state.

Key Qualities of Resilient People

- **Adaptability**: Willingness to change plans and expectations when needed.
- **Optimism**: Confidence that challenges can be overcome, even if the path is not obvious at first.

- **Self-Compassion**: Being kind to yourself during struggles instead of harshly judging mistakes.
- **Persistence**: Continuing forward despite setbacks, one step at a time.

Building these qualities does not mean you never feel pain or disappointment. It means you recognize these emotions, work through them, and grow stronger instead of getting stuck in constant overthinking.

---

2. The Link Between Resilience and Overthinking

Overthinking often arises when you feel uncertain, scared of failure, or worried about the future. If your resilience is low, you might see every obstacle as a looming crisis. Strong resilience, however, helps you trust your ability to cope with whatever happens next. This trust prevents you from diving into endless "what if" questions and worst-case scenarios.

Example

Imagine two people who lose their jobs unexpectedly:

- **Person A (Low Resilience)**: They immediately fall into panic. They think, "I'll never find another job. I can't handle this!" They replay the situation in their mind for weeks, losing sleep and becoming convinced of a bleak future.
- **Person B (High Resilience)**: They feel upset, but after some initial frustration, they say, "This is tough, but I've handled tough things before. Let me update my resume, look for new opportunities, and maybe explore a different field." They still feel stress, but they focus on practical steps rather than getting trapped in gloom.

Person B's resilience does not remove the hardship, but it keeps them from overthinking and taking the situation as a permanent defeat.

---

3. Core Components of Emotional Resilience

Building resilience involves several core components, each of which can be nurtured and strengthened:

3.1 Self-Awareness

Understanding your emotional responses helps you see when you start to spiral into worry. The previous chapters on awareness and identifying triggers feed directly into this component. The more aware you are of your feelings, the more quickly you can take corrective action.

3.2 Acceptance of Change

Life is always moving. People change, jobs change, and even your interests evolve. If you resist change too strongly, you might cling to old situations and overthink every variation from the norm. Learning to see change as natural can ease the fear that fuels overthinking.

3.3 Sense of Purpose

Having a broader goal or direction in life can motivate you to push past setbacks. This could be a career path, a personal value system, or a passion for something like art or community service. When faced with challenges, remembering your "why" provides a stable anchor.

3.4 Healthy Support System

No one is entirely self-reliant. A strong network of friends, family, or mentors offers emotional support. This makes you less likely to feel alone when problems arise, reducing the urge to overthink in isolation.

---

4. Strategies for Building Emotional Resilience

4.1 Practice Positive Self-Talk

In Chapter 6, we discussed how to create helpful thought patterns. This is central to resilience. Telling yourself, "I can't do this," weakens your resolve. Replacing that with "I'll learn as I go" strengthens your mindset. If you repeatedly feed your brain supportive words, it becomes more natural to bounce back when life tests you.

4.2 Focus on What You Can Control

Overthinking often involves worrying about things outside your control—like other people's opinions or unexpected events. Instead, direct your attention to what you can do right now: sending out job applications, practicing new skills, or reaching out for advice. This shift in focus from uncontrollable factors to manageable tasks fosters a sense of competence.

4.3 Set Realistic Goals

Big, lofty goals are fine, but breaking them into smaller steps can reduce anxiety and build resilience. When you see yourself achieving these smaller milestones, it boosts confidence and shows you are moving forward, despite obstacles.

4.4 Cultivate Flexible Thinking

As we learned, rigid thinking—believing there is only one solution—leads to crisis if that solution fails. Flexible thinking invites multiple paths. If Plan A fails, you are mentally prepared to try Plan B or C without slipping into endless worry.

4.5 Celebrate Small Wins

Resilience grows each time you acknowledge your successes. It might be something small like finishing a challenging task or speaking up in a meeting when you are usually shy. Over time, these wins add up, reinforcing the idea that you are capable of overcoming bumps in the road.

5. Handling Adversity Without Overthinking

5.1 Reframing Failure

Failure is often viewed as a final verdict on your abilities, which fuels negative self-talk. But what if you see failure as a lesson? Each time something does not go as planned, ask yourself: "What can I learn?" "How will this help me next time?" By adopting a learning mindset, you transform setbacks into stepping stones instead of mental roadblocks.

5.2 Emotional Processing

If you lose a job or end a relationship, it is natural to feel sadness or disappointment. Resilience is not about avoiding these emotions but allowing yourself to feel them without letting them consume you. Journaling, talking to someone you trust, or even spending a few quiet moments acknowledging the pain can all help you process emotions in a healthy way.

5.3 Avoiding the Overthinking Trap

- **Time-Limited Reflection**: Give yourself a set period—maybe 30 minutes—to analyze what went wrong. After that, move on to action or rest.
- **Seek Perspective**: Talk with a friend or mentor to see the situation more objectively. Overthinking often thrives on isolation, so an outside viewpoint can balance things out.
- **Plan Next Steps**: Once emotions calm a bit, outline one or two practical actions. This keeps you from circling the same thoughts endlessly.

---

6. Building Self-Compassion

Resilience requires kindness toward yourself, especially when things go badly. Overthinkers often judge themselves harshly, blaming their own "weakness" for mistakes. This only deepens negative cycles. Self-compassion involves treating yourself as you would a dear friend—acknowledging you are human and will make mistakes.

Simple Ways to Practice Self-Compassion

- **Positive Mirror Talk**: Look in the mirror and say one supportive phrase to yourself each day.
- **Write a Self-Compassion Letter**: Imagine you are writing to a friend going through your exact problem, offering empathy. Then realize you deserve that same empathy.
- **List Personal Strengths**: When you feel down, remind yourself of what you do well—kindness, persistence, creativity, etc.

---

7. Emotional Intelligence and Resilience

Emotional intelligence (EI) is the ability to recognize, understand, and manage both your own emotions and those of others. People with high EI tend to be more resilient because they respond to challenges with clear, balanced thinking rather than letting raw emotions take over.

Components of EI

1. **Self-Awareness**: Recognizing your own emotions and how they affect your thoughts and behavior.
2. **Self-Regulation**: Being able to control impulsive feelings and actions, staying calm under pressure.
3. **Motivation**: Using passion to reach goals, even when faced with setbacks.
4. **Empathy**: Understanding and being sensitive to the feelings of others.
5. **Social Skills**: Communicating effectively and building strong relationships.

If you improve these areas, you naturally enhance your resilience. You become better at handling stress, cooperating with others during tough times, and staying hopeful when you might otherwise spiral into overthinking.

8. The Role of Boundaries in Resilience

Having clear personal boundaries is a key piece of emotional health. Boundaries define what you find acceptable in relationships, work, and personal time. Without them, you might take on too many responsibilities or let others' demands drive you into mental fatigue, making it harder to stay resilient.

How to Strengthen Boundaries

1. **Identify Limits**: Be honest about how much work, socializing, or emotional care you can handle.
2. **Communicate Clearly**: If you need personal time or if a coworker's behavior bothers you, politely let them know.
3. **Learn to Say No**: It is not selfish to protect your well-being by declining tasks you cannot comfortably handle.
4. **Accept Consequences**: Some people may react poorly to new boundaries. Maintain them anyway for the sake of your mental health.

Once you have healthier boundaries, you reduce avoidable stress. This frees up mental energy, making it easier to bounce back from the challenges you cannot avoid.

---

9. Nurturing Support Systems

No one thrives in isolation, especially when going through hardships. A supportive circle of friends, family, or mentors can be a pillar of resilience. If you do not have strong support at home, you can find community groups, online forums, or professional counselors.

Healthy Communication

- **Share Your Feelings**: Let trusted people know when you are struggling. You might be surprised how willing they are to help or listen.
- **Be a Support, Too**: Resilience grows when you help others, as well. Encouraging a friend can remind you of your own strengths.

- **Avoid Toxic Influences**: People who constantly criticize or dismiss your feelings can lower your resilience. Consider limiting contact or setting firm boundaries with them.

---

10. Maintaining a Growth Mindset

Stanford psychologist Carol Dweck coined the term "growth mindset," which means believing your abilities and intelligence can be developed through dedication and effort. In contrast, a "fixed mindset" assumes your traits are unchangeable. A growth mindset is closely linked to resilience because it frames failures and obstacles as part of the learning process, not a final verdict on who you are.

Encouraging a Growth Mindset

- **Look for Lessons**: Each setback or mistake teaches you something valuable if you look for it.
- **Embrace Challenges**: Instead of avoiding difficult tasks, see them as opportunities to push your limits.
- **Reward Effort, Not Just Outcome**: Praise yourself (and others) for hard work, perseverance, or new ideas, rather than only celebrating end results.

---

11. Practical Exercises for Building Resilience

11.1 Daily Reflection on Strengths

At the end of each day, write down one thing you did well—no matter how small. This habit shifts your focus from what went wrong to what went right, boosting your confidence.

11.2 "Worst-Case / Best-Case / Most-Likely" Analysis

When faced with a problem:

- **Worst-Case**: Allow yourself to imagine the absolute worst outcome.
- **Best-Case**: Then imagine the ideal scenario where everything goes perfectly.
- **Most-Likely**: Finally, note what is realistically probable.

This exercise reminds you that while bad outcomes are possible, they are often not the only option. In many cases, reality lands somewhere in between.

11.3 Stress Inoculation

Gradually expose yourself to manageable levels of stress to build tolerance. For instance, if you fear public speaking, start by talking in front of a small group of friends, then step up to slightly larger audiences. With each successful experience, you increase resilience and reduce the mental chatter of "I can't do this."

---

12. Overcoming Major Life Setbacks

Some events—like losing a loved one, going through a divorce, or facing a serious illness—can test your resilience to the maximum. During these times, your goal is not to avoid pain, but to navigate it without losing hope.

Seeking Professional Help

Counselors, therapists, or support groups can be invaluable during major crises. They provide a safe space to process intense emotions and learn new coping strategies. Seeking help is a sign of strength, not weakness.

Giving Yourself Time

Big losses or changes can require weeks, months, or even years to fully heal. Patience is key. You may have days when you feel almost back to normal and days when grief resurfaces. Recognize this as part of the healing process instead of proof of failure.

Finding Meaning in Struggle

Some people discover a deeper sense of purpose after major challenges. They might use their experience to help others in similar situations or realize new values, like appreciating life's small joys. This sense of meaning can be a powerful driver of resilience, reminding you that there can be a silver lining even in dark times.

---

13. Conclusion

Emotional resilience is the strong, flexible framework that allows you to adapt and recover when life throws challenges your way. It does not prevent all pain or negativity, but it ensures those difficulties do not define you or trap you in overthinking. By nurturing qualities like self-awareness, positive self-talk, and a growth mindset, you equip yourself with the mental tools needed to bounce back from setbacks.

When you pair resilience with the calming techniques from the previous chapter, you create a robust defense against chronic worry and anxiety. Rather than letting fear or doubt consume your thoughts, you acknowledge them, learn from them, and move forward. This approach frees your mental space for creativity, joy, and purposeful action.

In the next chapters, we will look more closely at creating daily routines for mental clarity, understanding the link between physical health and mental well-being, and learning specific ways to handle stress and anxiety. With each new step, you add another layer of support for a mind that remains steady, even when tested.

Chapter 9: Habits and Routines for Mental Clarity

Introduction

We have covered recognizing triggers, creating helpful thought patterns, calming the mind, and developing emotional resilience. Now, let's take a deeper look at everyday habits and routines. Building a steady structure into your day can reduce mental noise because it lowers uncertainty. You know what to expect, and your mind does not waste energy wondering what to do next. Simple routines—from how you start your morning to how you finish your evening—can act like anchors that keep you from drifting into overthinking.

In this chapter, we will talk about which habits can help clear your mind, how to structure your day effectively, and ways to maintain these routines in the long run. By the end, you will see that clarity often emerges from stable, predictable daily rhythms that support a peaceful mind and balanced emotions.

---

1. Why Habits Matter

A habit is a behavior we do regularly, often without conscious thought. When you brush your teeth in the morning, you do not spend ten minutes deciding if you should or should not. You simply do it. Building beneficial habits allows your brain to run on "autopilot" for tasks that support your mental and physical health. This means fewer decisions, less stress, and more mental clarity.

Overthinkers often exhaust their brain by making choices over and over—"Should I do this now or later?" "Should I start with that task or the other?" When your life has reliable habits, some of these choices get made in advance. You reduce the mental clutter, freeing up headspace to focus on what truly matters.

Decision Fatigue

Decision fatigue happens when you face too many choices in a day and grow tired. You might find that by evening, small decisions—like what to cook for dinner—feel overwhelming. Habits and routines cut down on these small stressors. If you know that dinner is planned, you do not waste energy fretting about it, which helps preserve your mental clarity.

2. Identifying Your Prime Times

Each of us has certain times of day when our minds and bodies feel more energized. Some people are "morning larks," alert and focused right after sunrise. Others are "night owls," finding their creative spark in the evening. Pay attention to when you naturally feel your best. You can schedule your most challenging or creative tasks during these high-energy windows. Conversely, plan simpler or less demanding activities for times when you typically feel low on energy.

Tracking Energy Levels

Try keeping a short log for a week. Every couple of hours, write down how awake and focused you feel on a scale of 1–10. Look for patterns. If you find your score is consistently high from 8–10 a.m. but dips around 2 p.m., that suggests you should handle key tasks early and perhaps take a short break or do routine chores in the afternoon. Adapting your schedule to your natural rhythms can lessen overthinking since you are not pushing your brain to work at times it resists.

3. Designing a Morning Routine

How you start your day often sets the tone for everything that follows. A chaotic morning—rushing out the door, missing breakfast, and forgetting important items—can put you in a frantic mindset. Overthinkers might begin worrying about the day's challenges before they have even fully woken up. A structured morning routine provides a gentle, organized start.

Possible Elements of a Calm Morning Routine

1. **Wake-Up at a Consistent Time**
   Choosing a regular wake-up hour helps regulate your internal body clock. You feel more rested over time, and you do not lie in bed overthinking about whether to sleep longer.
2. **Brief Mindful Practice**
   Take a minute or two to do deep breathing or light stretching. This transitions you from sleep to wakefulness in a calm manner.
3. **Hydration and Nutrition**
   Drink a glass of water soon after waking. If time allows, have a balanced breakfast. Fueling your body prevents energy dips later, which can trigger anxious thoughts.
4. **Review Your Day's Plan**
   Look at your schedule or to-do list. Avoid analyzing it in extreme detail. Simply confirm the main tasks or events. This helps you feel prepared without spinning into overthinking.
5. **Avoid Immediate Digital Overload**
   Checking emails or social media in bed can spark worry before you have grounded yourself. If possible, wait until after breakfast or at least a few minutes into your morning to look at your phone.

Over time, these small steps create a sense of control and calm right from the start of the day. You begin feeling purposeful, lowering the odds that anxious thoughts will take over.

---

4. Structuring Your Work or School Day

The middle of the day is often when responsibilities pile up—meetings, homework, errands, and more. Without structure, tasks can seem jumbled, fueling stress and making it easier to slip into overthinking.

Task Prioritization

Make a habit of identifying your top two or three priorities for the day. Focus on completing them first, rather than trying to tackle a dozen items at once. Having fewer priorities can reduce mental clutter. If you finish them early, then you can move on to secondary tasks. This method, sometimes called the "MITs" approach (Most Important Tasks), forces you to be realistic about what you can handle and stops you from worrying about every small item on your list.

Work or Study Blocks

Try segmenting your day into blocks of focused work or study, followed by short breaks. For instance, work intently for 25 minutes, then take a 5-minute break (the Pomodoro Technique). During these breaks, stretch, walk around, or take a few deep breaths. This cycle allows your brain to rest briefly before diving back in. It also lowers the risk of drifting into a worrying state because you know a short pause is coming soon.

Reducing Distractions

If possible, find a quiet space or use noise-cancelling headphones. Turn off non-essential phone notifications or place your phone face-down. Each time you check messages or social media, you risk triggering anxious or distracting thoughts—especially if you see something stressful. By controlling these external distractions, you keep your mental space clearer.

---

5. The Power of Breaks and Downtime

Many people think they should always be busy to be productive. In reality, short breaks can greatly boost efficiency and help maintain a calm mind. If you do not pause, tension can build up until you are overwhelmed.

Midday Mindfulness

Taking just two minutes in the middle of the day to close your eyes and breathe can reset your mental state. Go for a quick walk outside, or if you cannot leave your desk, simply stretch and look away from your screen. Doing so prevents your thoughts from racing unchecked.

Importance of Lunchtime

Skipping lunch or eating while working can increase stress. Mealtime is a natural breakpoint. By treating lunch as a mini-reset, you give your brain and body a moment to recharge. That helps you approach the afternoon with a fresh perspective.

---

6. Building an Evening Routine

Just as a morning routine provides a calm start, an evening routine helps you wind down. If you go straight from working or studying to trying to sleep, your mind might still be racing with thoughts about the day's events or tomorrow's worries.

Ideas for an Evening Routine

1. **Set a "Wrap-Up" Time**
   Pick a time to stop checking work emails or thinking about tomorrow's tasks. This signals your brain that it is time to shift from "doing" to "resting."
2. **Light Organization**
   Spend a few minutes tidying up your environment. Put away clutter, wash dishes, or organize your desk. A neat space can ease anxious thoughts, especially in the morning.
3. **Relaxing Activity**
   Engage in something enjoyable but not too stimulating—like reading a light book, drawing, or listening to calm music. Avoid intense shows or heavy news right before bed.
4. **Low or No Screen Time**
   The blue light from devices can disrupt sleep. If possible, limit phone or computer use an hour before bedtime. If you must use a screen, consider wearing blue-light-blocking glasses or using a night-mode filter.
5. **Short Reflection or Gratitude**
   End your day by noting one or two things you appreciated about the day. This gentle reflection counters negative loops and helps you feel more settled.

7. Weekly and Monthly Check-Ins

While daily habits are vital, it is also helpful to step back once a week or month for a broader reflection. Consider scheduling a weekly check-in with yourself, maybe on a Sunday evening. Review your major goals, see what went well, and note where you struggled. This is not meant to spark self-criticism; instead, treat it as a chance to adjust your habits. If you notice you overthink a lot on Mondays, for example, you might tweak your Monday routine to include extra mindfulness or fewer commitments.

Over a month, you might assess whether your current routines still serve you. Maybe you started a new hobby that shifted your schedule, or a new job changed your best times for focus. These check-ins keep your habits aligned with your life as it evolves.

---

8. Routines Outside of Work and School

Habits are not just about productivity; they also cover personal and social parts of life. Overthinking can creep into relationships, hobbies, and leisure time if these areas lack structure.

Social Routines

If you tend to worry about meeting friends or dread last-minute invites, consider planning regular meetups. For instance, set a standing date every Wednesday evening with a close friend. That predictability can reduce social anxiety and the mental back-and-forth of scheduling. You know your calendar, and you do not have to overthink it.

Leisure Routines

Free time is essential, but if you are prone to overthinking, unstructured free time can turn into hours of worry. A balanced approach is to have a few go-to hobbies or relaxation activities—reading, painting, jogging—so you know what you can do to unwind. This does not mean you schedule every moment of your free time, but having a gentle plan or favorite fallback activity can help stop anxious overanalyzing about "How should I spend my downtime?"

9. The Role of Flexibility in Routines

Routines should serve you, not trap you. Strictly following a routine if it causes stress or guilt can lead to a new form of overthinking: "I messed up my schedule—I'm a failure!" Life changes, and unexpected events come up. Flexibility allows you to adapt without feeling you have lost control.

Balancing Routine and Adaptability

1. **Allow Wiggle Room**: Schedule tasks with some buffer time. If you plan to exercise at 6 p.m. but get stuck in traffic until 6:30, try not to stress. Maybe your workout is shorter or rescheduled.
2. **Accept Occasional Breaks**: If you miss a day of journaling or do not follow your routine perfectly, that is okay. Consistency is a goal, not an absolute rule.
3. **Regularly Reassess**: If a routine feels more draining than helpful, modify it. Maybe a morning person tries to force late-night study sessions, leading to fatigue and worry. Adjust your schedule to match your strengths.

Embracing a gentle approach helps you enjoy the benefits of routine without it becoming another source of anxiety.

10. Overcoming Common Barriers to Building Routines

It is normal to face hurdles when establishing new habits. Being aware of these challenges can help you plan for them.

10.1 Procrastination

You might decide to create a better morning routine but keep putting it off. Consider starting with very small steps—like setting an earlier alarm by just ten minutes instead of an hour. Gradual changes are easier to maintain.

10.2 Lack of Motivation

Sometimes, you do not feel like sticking to the schedule. Remind yourself why you want these routines: to reduce overthinking, boost focus, and create a calmer life. Having a clear "why" can push you through low-motivation days.

10.3 Distractions and Interruptions

Maybe your family or roommates have different schedules, or you have unpredictable work demands. Be patient. Try to carve out small windows you can control and let others know about your plans if possible. They may be willing to help you keep a consistent routine.

10.4 Self-Criticism

If you slip up, watch out for harsh thoughts like "I'll never keep a routine." Instead, acknowledge the slip and keep going. Habit-building is not a straight line; it is more like a winding path with ups and downs.

---

11. Tools and Techniques to Maintain Habits

Now that we have explored different routines, let us talk about how to stick with them over the long haul. Many find that short-term motivation fades, so having reliable tools is key.

Habit Trackers

A habit tracker can be as simple as a paper checklist or a note on your phone. You record each day's habit completion—whether that is meditating, journaling, or a quick stretch routine. Seeing a streak can be motivating and gives you a clear view of your progress.

Alarms and Reminders

Use your phone or a calendar app to remind you of important tasks until they become second nature. If you want to read every evening, set a gentle notification 30 minutes before bedtime. This reminder helps you transition from daily tasks to reading time without allowing overthinking to sabotage the plan.

Accountability Buddy

Working on routines with a friend or family member can help. Share daily or weekly check-ins about your progress. If you slip up, they might provide encouragement or tips to get back on track. Similarly, you can support them in their goals.

---

12. Sustaining Mental Clarity Through Routines

When done well, habits and routines can drastically cut down on stress and mental chatter. Instead of waking up each day full of "what ifs," you wake up to a stable outline of what you will do, how you will do it, and approximately when. This stability does not eliminate life's surprises—no routine can. But it does provide a foundation that helps you navigate those surprises with less anxiety.

By spreading your energy across predictable tasks throughout the day and week, you keep your mind calm and your emotions balanced. In moments when overthinking tries to sneak in, you can lean on your established rhythms, knowing you have a plan and do not have to figure everything out at once. Over time, living with structured habits becomes part of who you are, allowing your mental clarity to grow naturally.

13. Conclusion

Creating routines is not about becoming rigid or losing spontaneity. It is about giving your mind and body a supportive framework so they do not have to manage chaos all the time. By carefully planning small habits—like a consistent wake-up time, setting priorities for the day, taking short mindful breaks, and winding down at night—you give yourself daily pockets of calm. These habits act as guardrails, keeping you from veering off into unproductive worry.

Moreover, routines help you realize you have more control over your life than you might think. This sense of control reduces stress, increases confidence, and allows space for creativity and fun. In the next chapter, we will explore the critical link between physical health and mental well-being. After all, habits around sleep, diet, and exercise play a huge part in preventing or managing overthinking. By merging consistent routines with a healthy body, you can truly thrive.

Chapter 10: The Role of Physical Health in Reducing Overthinking

Introduction

Our minds and bodies are closely connected. If your body is under stress—tired, malnourished, or inactive—your brain is more likely to wander into anxious thoughts. In earlier chapters, we focused primarily on mental and emotional strategies to manage overthinking. But physical health can make a remarkable difference, too. A well-rested, well-nourished body often supports clearer thinking, better emotional balance, and greater resilience.

In this chapter, we will examine how factors like sleep, nutrition, exercise, and overall lifestyle contribute to a calmer mind. You will learn why small changes in physical habits can lower stress hormones and reduce the urge to overthink. We will also cover practical steps for improving daily habits so you can see real benefits in your mental clarity.

---

1. The Mind-Body Connection

For thousands of years, people have recognized that physical well-being impacts mental well-being. Modern science has added specifics: hormones, neurotransmitters, and the nervous system all link mind and body. If you regularly experience tension, lack of sleep, or poor diet, your body produces stress hormones like cortisol, which can trigger or worsen anxious thinking.

Why Stress Physically Affects Thoughts

When the body senses stress, it prepares for "fight or flight." This state can help you react to danger quickly, but it also narrows your mental focus. You become hyper-aware of threats, real or imagined. Overthinkers may interpret everyday issues—like a messy desk or an upcoming test—as major dangers. By keeping your body healthier, you reduce the baseline stress response, making it less likely that you will spiral into overthinking.

2. Sleep: The Foundation of Mental Health

One of the most significant factors that affect overthinking is sleep quality and duration. A tired brain has a harder time regulating emotions and a weaker ability to fend off negative or racing thoughts.

Consequences of Sleep Deprivation

- **Impaired Memory**: You might forget tasks or facts, leading to more anxiety about performance.
- **Lower Mood**: Lack of sleep can contribute to irritability or sadness, which can fuel overthinking.
- **Reduced Focus**: With less concentration, you might spend more time worrying or re-checking tasks.
- **Higher Stress Levels**: The body produces more cortisol when sleep is lacking, creating a cycle of anxiety and unrest.

Strategies for Better Sleep

1. **Consistent Schedule**: Go to bed and wake up around the same time, even on weekends.
2. **Pre-Sleep Routine**: Dim lights, read a calming book, or do gentle stretches. This signals your body to wind down.
3. **Limit Caffeine and Screens**: Both can disrupt sleep if used late in the day.
4. **Comfortable Environment**: Keep your bedroom cool, dark, and quiet if possible.

When you regularly get enough restful sleep, you strengthen your mental foundation, making it easier to ward off overthinking patterns.

---

3. Nutrition: Fueling a Clear Mind

What you eat can significantly influence your mental state. While occasional treats are fine, a habit of consuming too much sugar or junk food can lead to energy crashes that open the door to anxious thoughts. On the other hand, balanced meals containing vitamins, minerals, healthy fats, and proteins can help stabilize blood sugar and mood.

Key Nutritional Tips

1. **Balanced Meals**: Aim for a mix of protein (e.g., lean meats, beans, tofu), complex carbs (e.g., whole grains, vegetables), and healthy fats (e.g., avocados, nuts).
2. **Stay Hydrated**: Mild dehydration can trigger fatigue and irritability. Drink water consistently throughout the day.
3. **Limit Sugar Spikes**: Large amounts of refined sugars can cause rapid spikes, then crashes, in energy, often followed by restlessness or fuzzy thinking.
4. **Consider Whole Foods**: Generally, less-processed foods provide more consistent nutrients and tend to avoid additives that may affect mood or energy.

Caffeine and Overthinking

Caffeine, found in coffee, tea, and many sodas, can be useful for alertness. However, it also revs up your nervous system, potentially feeding anxiety and sleeplessness if consumed in large amounts or late in the day. If you are prone to overthinking, moderate your caffeine intake and see how you feel. Reducing or cutting back caffeine can lessen jitters and nighttime racing thoughts.

---

4. Exercise and Movement

Physical activity is a powerful tool for mental health. Exercise stimulates the release of endorphins—often called "feel-good" chemicals—that help stabilize mood and reduce stress. It also provides a healthy outlet for pent-up energy, which could otherwise fuel anxious thinking.

Types of Exercise for a Calmer Mind

1. **Cardio Workouts**: Running, brisk walking, cycling, or swimming get your heart rate up. They often help burn off tension and worry.
2. **Strength Training**: Lifting weights or doing bodyweight exercises not only builds muscle but also boosts confidence and self-esteem.

3. **Yoga or Pilates**: These gentle forms of movement focus on mindfulness and controlled breathing, ideal for quieting an overactive mind.
4. **Simple Daily Movement**: Even short walks or dancing in your living room can help release stress.

Scheduling Exercise

Try short, regular activity instead of one big workout each week. Even 20 minutes of moderate activity a few times a week can make a difference. Experiment with the timing—some people feel calmer exercising in the morning, while others prefer the evening to burn off the day's worries.

5. The Impact of Stress Hormones

When you remain in a state of chronic stress, your body releases cortisol and adrenaline repeatedly. This can overload your system, leading to anxiety, overthinking, and physical symptoms like headaches or digestive issues. Healthy daily habits—sleeping well, eating balanced meals, exercising—naturally keep these hormones in check.

Learning to Downshift

Even short relaxation breaks can lower stress hormone levels:

- **Deep breathing** for a minute or two
- **Brief mindfulness** of your surroundings
- **Progressive muscle relaxation** in your chair

When done regularly, these tiny resets can prevent stress from piling up to the point where overthinking becomes a natural response.

6. Managing Substances That Influence the Mind

Beyond caffeine, other substances like alcohol or nicotine can also affect your mental state. Some people turn to alcohol to unwind, but it can disturb sleep quality and worsen mood the next day. Nicotine, found in cigarettes or vapes, provides a temporary feeling of relief but can increase stress and anxiety over time as the body craves more.

Alcohol and Overthinking

Alcohol can act as a depressant, dulling anxiety for a short period. However, it often rebounds into increased worry or low mood as it leaves your system. If you notice that a few drinks make you more prone to restless thoughts or a poor night's sleep, it may be worth cutting back or seeking alternatives to de-stress.

Smoking or Vaping

Nicotine speeds up your heart rate and can make your nerves jittery. Some smokers feel more anxious when they cannot smoke, leading to a cycle of tension and temporary relief. Quitting or reducing smoking can lower overall stress in the long run, which in turn can reduce overthinking.

---

7. Creating a Supportive Environment

Your surroundings—home, workplace, or even the community—affect your mental well-being. Clutter, noise, or constant interruptions can fuel tension and lead your mind to fixate on problems or details.

Tips for a Calm Physical Space

1. **Declutter Regularly**: Piles of paperwork or random objects can overwhelm your senses. A tidy environment often means a tidier mind.
2. **Bring in Nature**: Plants, flowers, or even nature photographs can create a soothing atmosphere.
3. **Adjust Lighting**: Harsh, bright lights in the evening can disrupt sleep cues. Use softer lighting or lamps when winding down.

4. **Manage Noise Levels**: Earplugs or noise-cancelling headphones can help if you live in a noisy area. Alternatively, gentle background music or nature sounds might relax you.

Ergonomics and Comfort

If you work at a desk for long hours, investing in a comfortable chair or properly positioned monitor can reduce physical tension that might slip into mental stress. Simple adjustments—like placing your keyboard at the right height—can have an impact on how tense you feel physically, which then affects your mindset.

---

8. Combining Healthy Routines for Maximum Effect

Physical health is not just one thing; it is a combination of many small habits woven into daily life. Each piece—sleep, diet, exercise, and environment—works together. Improving even one area can support the others. For example, if you start exercising regularly, you may sleep better. Better sleep can lead to better food choices the next day, which can keep your energy steady, reducing anxious thoughts.

Creating a Balanced Daily Schedule

Here is a sample structure that integrates physical health with mental clarity:

- **Morning**: Wake up at a consistent time; light stretch or short walk; a balanced breakfast.
- **Midday**: Healthy lunch with a mix of protein and veggies; short walk during lunch break or do a mini workout if possible.
- **Afternoon Break**: Quick snack (like fruit or nuts) and a few deep breaths or mindful minutes.
- **Evening**: Light dinner (avoid heavy, greasy foods close to bedtime); reduce screen time; short, relaxing activity.

- **Bedtime**: Wind down with calming music or reading; lights dimmed; aim for 7–9 hours of sleep.

If a perfectly structured schedule every day sounds unrealistic, that is okay. Consistency is the goal, but occasional deviations happen. Focus on building a sustainable routine that supports both body and mind.

---

9. Overcoming Barriers to Better Physical Health

Sometimes, people want to improve their physical routines but face obstacles.

9.1 Time Constraints

A busy job, school demands, or family responsibilities can limit how much time you have. Solutions might include:

- Short workouts at home (10- or 15-minute routines).
- Meal prepping on weekends.
- Taking "walking meetings" or stretching during phone calls.

9.2 Budget Challenges

Healthy living does not have to be expensive. Many bodyweight exercises (push-ups, squats) are free, as are walks in the park. Nutritious foods can be affordable if you focus on basics like beans, rice, eggs, and seasonal vegetables. Planning meals can help cut down on costly takeout or processed snacks.

9.3 Lack of Motivation

If you find yourself unmotivated, remind yourself of the mental benefits you stand to gain. A calmer mind, fewer racing thoughts, and better emotional stability can be powerful reasons to stick with healthier habits.

9.4 Social Pressures

Friends or family might not share your goals. They might encourage late nights or junk food. While occasional indulgences are fine, kindly communicate your reasons for wanting to keep a healthier schedule. Ask for their support or at least for them not to discourage you. Sometimes, you might find a buddy who wants to join you in adopting better habits.

---

10. Tracking Progress and Staying Consistent

As with building any routine, monitoring your progress can help you stay on track. Keep a simple record of your sleep hours, meals, and exercise for a week or two. Notice changes in your mood or in how often you slip into overthinking. You might be surprised at how much better you feel just by regularly getting enough sleep or adding a daily walk.

Reward Systems

Give yourself small rewards for meeting goals—like completing a week of good sleep habits or hitting a new exercise milestone. This could be treating yourself to a fun outing or a new book. Positive reinforcement can keep you motivated and remind you of the link between physical self-care and mental peace.

---

11. Handling Setbacks

Change rarely happens without bumps in the road. Maybe you get sick and cannot exercise for a week, or you face a busy season at work and end up sleeping less. Try not to let setbacks turn into self-criticism or an excuse to give up. Restart when you can. Each attempt at a healthier lifestyle teaches you something about what works and what does not, helping you refine your approach.

Learning from Mistakes

If a certain diet plan left you exhausted or a workout schedule was too intense, adjust it. The goal is sustainable improvements, not short bursts of perfection. Ask yourself what went wrong: Was it timing? Over-ambition? Outside factors? With answers in hand, modify your plan and keep going.

12. Holistic Wellness and Overthinking

Physical health is one pillar of wellness, but it connects to other pillars like mental and emotional well-being, social connections, and a sense of purpose. Building a lifestyle that respects all these areas creates a strong foundation where overthinking has less room to grow. If you combine the techniques from earlier chapters—like mindfulness, journaling, and resilience-building—with a balanced physical routine, you create a powerful support system for your mind.

Helping Others, Helping Yourself

Sometimes, focusing on physical health alongside friends or family can boost your own adherence. Whether it is cooking healthy meals together or scheduling group activities, having companionship can make it more enjoyable. Plus, encouraging others to take care of themselves can reinforce your own commitment.

13. Conclusion

Physical health is not a quick fix for all mental challenges, but it is a core part of a balanced life that reduces the likelihood of overthinking. When your body is running on good sleep, nutritious food, and regular movement, your mind has fewer reasons to jump into anxiety or rumination. You feel steadier, more in tune with your own needs, and better equipped to handle stress.

This chapter showed you practical ways to improve sleep habits, nutrition, exercise routines, and your environment. Start with small changes. Over time, these adjustments can lead to significant improvements in mood, concentration, and overall mental well-being. In the next set of chapters, we will dive deeper into specific methods to deal with stress and anxiety—further building on your growing toolbox of strategies for quieting your mind and cultivating a focused, peaceful life.

Chapter 11: Dealing with Anxiety and Stress

Introduction

While overthinking and anxiety are closely linked, they are not exactly the same. Overthinking is mostly about mental loops—repetitive thoughts that do not lead to solutions. Anxiety can include these thoughts, but it also involves a physical and emotional reaction to stress or fear. When you feel anxious, you might sense a racing heart or tense muscles, along with a deep worry that something bad will happen.

In this chapter, we will explore how anxiety and stress feed into overthinking, discuss the difference between healthy and unhealthy levels of stress, and present practical techniques to handle anxiety before it grows out of control. You will learn how to manage daily stressors in ways that keep your mind calm and prevent unnecessary cycles of rumination.

---

1. Understanding Anxiety

Anxiety is a natural human emotion. In small doses, it signals that something needs your attention. For instance, mild anxiety before a test may push you to study, while mild anxiety about finances can prompt you to be more careful with spending. The problem arises when anxiety becomes too intense or sticks around for too long, draining your mental energy and leading to constant worry.

Signs of Anxiety

- **Physical Sensations**: Racing heart, sweating, trembling, stomach knots, and shortness of breath.
- **Mental Patterns**: Expecting the worst outcome, or feeling trapped by repetitive worries about the future.

- **Behavioral Changes**: Avoiding certain people or places to dodge stressful situations, or constantly seeking reassurance from others.

Anxiety can also turn into a cycle. You feel anxious, then your mind looks for reasons to justify the anxiety, leading to more worry. This can eventually build into overthinking, where thoughts loop over the same fears or "what if" scenarios.

---

2. Stress: The Good, the Bad, and the Overwhelming

Stress is your body's reaction to challenging events or demands. A little stress can be beneficial—like a spark of energy to meet a deadline or handle an emergency. But continuous high stress taxes your body and mind, which may lead to anxiety or burnout.

Types of Stress

1. **Acute Stress**: A short burst of tension or excitement, such as giving a speech or facing a tight project deadline. It subsides once the event passes.
2. **Episodic Acute Stress**: When acute stress happens frequently, like constantly rushing or always feeling pressed for time.
3. **Chronic Stress**: Long-term stress that persists day after day—like a difficult job or ongoing conflict at home. This is the most harmful type, as it can wear down your health and mental clarity.

When stress reaches a high enough level, it can trigger anxiety. The body releases hormones (like cortisol) to keep you in "fight or flight" mode. If this continues for too long, you may experience irritability, fatigue, and a greater tendency to overthink.

3. The Connection Between Overthinking, Anxiety, and Stress

Imagine a loop:

1. **Stressful Situation**: A big test, a work deadline, or money worries.
2. **Anxiety Response**: Your body goes on alert; your mind jumps to negative outcomes.
3. **Overthinking**: You replay fears, fueling more anxiety.
4. **Increased Stress**: Because you feel overwhelmed, your body remains tense, producing more anxious thoughts.

The good news is you can break this loop at various points—by handling stress more effectively, calming anxiety, or changing your thought patterns. As you keep practicing, you may notice anxious feelings do not last as long and overthinking becomes less frequent.

---

4. Short-Term Tools for Managing Anxiety

When anxiety strikes, you need quick, effective methods to bring your mind and body back to a calmer state. Think of these methods as a first-aid kit for anxious moments.

4.1 Deep Breathing Exercises

When your heart races, focus on slow, deliberate breaths. Inhale through your nose for a count of four, hold for one or two seconds, and exhale gently through your mouth for a count of four. Repeat this for a minute or two. By deliberately slowing your breathing, you signal your nervous system to calm down.

4.2 Grounding Techniques

Grounding methods help you shift your attention to the present, rather than scary "what if" scenarios:

- **5-4-3-2-1 Method**: Name five things you see, four things you can touch, three things you hear, two things you can smell, and one thing you can taste or remember the taste of.
- **Temperature Change**: Splash cold water on your face or hold an ice cube for a moment. The sudden sensation can pull you out of anxious thought loops.

4.3 Positive Distraction

If you are caught in worry, find a quick distraction that requires mental focus. This might be a puzzle game, doodling, or even a short conversation on a different topic. Distracting yourself for a few minutes can help the anxiety intensity drop so you can return to the issue with a clearer mind.

---

5. Longer-Term Strategies for Anxiety Reduction

While short-term fixes can provide quick relief, it is also important to develop habits that lower overall anxiety levels. As we have discussed in prior chapters, routines and self-awareness play big roles here. Additionally, you can adopt other strategies that boost your ability to handle stress.

5.1 Cognitive Behavioral Techniques

Cognitive Behavioral Therapy (CBT) is a common therapy approach for anxiety. Even if you do not see a therapist, you can practice certain CBT-inspired methods:

- **Identify the Thought**: Recognize the specific worry you are having (e.g., "I'm scared I'll fail my exam.").
- **Challenge the Thought**: Ask yourself, "Is there evidence this will definitely happen?" or "Could there be another outcome?"
- **Reframe**: Change your perspective. For example, "I have studied, and while I might not get a perfect score, I'm prepared enough to pass."

Over time, you teach your brain to pause and question anxious assumptions, reducing their power.

5.2 Creating a "Calm Corner"

Having a designated space at home to relax can help. This does not have to be big—maybe a comfy chair in a quiet corner with a soft light, a blanket, and a few items that help you feel safe (like a favorite book or calming artwork). When you feel anxiety creeping in, go to your "calm corner" and let yourself decompress for a few minutes.

5.3 Assertiveness and Boundaries

Sometimes anxiety comes from feeling out of control, or from taking on too many demands from others. Learning to set boundaries—like saying "no" when you need to or asking for help instead of trying to do everything alone—can lessen your load. Less stress means fewer sparks for anxiety, leading to less overthinking overall.

---

6. Handling Daily Stress to Prevent Anxiety

Not all stress can be eliminated, but you can often reduce it or manage how you respond. Handling stress in healthier ways keeps it from morphing into persistent anxiety.

6.1 Healthy Scheduling

If your calendar is overloaded, you constantly feel rushed. This stress can quickly spark anxiety. Try to:

- **Prioritize**: Identify your top tasks and focus on them first.
- **Delegate**: If possible, share responsibilities at work or home.
- **Plan Buffer Time**: Leave small gaps between tasks so you are not switching gears at breakneck speed.

6.2 Stress-Relieving Activities

In previous chapters, we discussed the power of exercise, hobbies, and social time. These activities reduce cortisol levels and boost endorphins, improving your stress tolerance. Whether it is jogging, painting, or cooking with friends, pick activities you truly enjoy so you are more likely to stick with them.

6.3 Digital Breaks

Constant notifications and online comparisons can feed stress. Try scheduling "digital-free" periods each day—maybe over lunch or an hour before bed. This break from social media and email can help your mind rest, making you less susceptible to anxious thoughts.

---

7. Recognizing Anxiety Disorders

Sometimes anxiety goes beyond normal stress. If you find anxiety or panic interfering with daily life—causing you to avoid work, friends, or routine activities—you may be dealing with an anxiety disorder. Common types include:

- **Generalized Anxiety Disorder (GAD)**: Ongoing, broad worry about many aspects of life.
- **Social Anxiety Disorder**: Intense fear of social situations or judgment by others.
- **Panic Disorder**: Frequent panic attacks—sudden surges of terror with strong physical symptoms.
- **Phobias**: Extreme fear focused on specific objects or situations (like heights, spiders, or flying).

If you suspect you have an anxiety disorder, consider talking to a mental health professional. Therapy, medication, or a combination of both can offer relief. There is no shame in seeking help; it can be the fastest route to regaining control of your life.

8. Self-Compassion When Anxiety Strikes

It is easy to feel disappointed in yourself when anxiety hits—"Why can't I handle this better?" However, self-criticism often worsens anxiety, leading to an added layer of shame. Instead, practice self-compassion:

- **Acknowledge the Feeling**: Say to yourself, "I'm anxious right now, and that's okay. It's a common human emotion."
- **Offer Kind Words**: Encourage yourself as you would a friend—"I know this is tough. I'm doing my best, and I will get through it."
- **Seek Support**: Talk to someone you trust about how you are feeling. Even a short text or call can make you feel less alone.

Self-compassion reminds you that anxiety is not a personal failing but a sign you need care and support.

---

9. Building an Anxiety-Resistant Lifestyle

The best approach to anxiety is a proactive one. By making consistent lifestyle choices that reduce stress and support emotional balance, you can create a strong foundation against anxious thoughts.

9.1 Physical Health

We covered this extensively in Chapter 10. Good sleep, a balanced diet, and regular exercise stabilize your body's stress response. A calmer body often equals a calmer mind.

9.2 Structured Routine

As described in Chapter 9, routines reduce uncertainty, leaving less room for anxious thoughts to take hold. A regular schedule for waking, sleeping, eating, and working helps you feel grounded.

9.3 Social Connections

Humans are social by nature. Positive relationships act as a buffer against stress, reminding you that you are not alone. Strong friendships or family ties can encourage you and offer perspectives you might not see on your own.

9.4 Mindful Presence

Chapter 12 will dive deeper into mindfulness, but here is a quick preview: staying present in the moment reduces the mental habit of worrying about future "what ifs." The more you practice mindful awareness, the more natural it becomes to let go of anxious loops.

---

10. Dealing with Setbacks

It is unrealistic to expect to never feel anxiety again. Setbacks happen—maybe an unexpected expense, a health scare, or a conflict at work triggers your worries. The key is how you respond.

10.1 Recognize the Early Signs

Often, anxiety creeps up slowly before hitting full force. Pay attention to smaller signs:

- A sudden, tight feeling in your chest
- Snapping at people more quickly
- Muscle aches or tension headaches becoming more frequent

When you notice these, apply your coping strategies immediately (deep breathing, grounding, or a quick break) rather than waiting for full-blown panic.

10.2 Revisit Your Tools

If anxiety worsens, review the methods we have discussed. Maybe you have slacked on exercise or cut back on sleep. If so, recommit to those habits. Or perhaps a certain grounding technique used to help but you have not tried it in a while. Pull it back into your daily routine.

10.3 Seek Extra Support

Sometimes you need more than self-help measures. If you are feeling overwhelmed, reach out—whether it is a friend, a family member, a counselor, or even a support group. Outside perspectives can remind you that your anxious thoughts are often magnified, not reflective of reality.

---

11. Anxiety in Specific Life Situations

Certain life phases can heighten anxiety—like starting college, beginning a new job, or becoming a parent. During these transitions, you may feel uncertain and overwhelmed. The methods we have covered—mindful breathing, self-compassion, structured routines—still apply, but you might also adapt them to your unique situation.

11.1 School or Work Anxiety

Deadlines, performance reviews, or big exams can spike stress levels. Try organizing a study group or a lunchtime walk with colleagues to break the tension. Recognize that occasional stress is normal, but if you feel constantly on edge, it might be time for a change in workload or a talk with a counselor.

11.2 Relationship Anxiety

Worries about rejection, conflict, or misunderstanding can fuel overthinking in personal relationships. Communicate openly with the other person instead of guessing what they feel or fear. Sharing your concerns calmly can clear up a lot of unknowns, reducing anxiety.

11.3 Health Anxiety

Some people fixate on physical symptoms, fearing serious illness. While checking with a doctor if you have concerns is wise, try not to obsessively search for every possible disease online. That habit often magnifies worry. If health anxiety becomes debilitating, a mental health professional can help you handle these fears more effectively.

12. Conclusion

Anxiety and stress are natural parts of life. They signal that something needs attention or change. In small doses, they can push us to grow or solve problems. But when they become intense or unrelenting, they trap us in cycles of overthinking. By understanding how stress triggers anxiety, learning coping strategies for anxious moments, and building a lifestyle that balances challenges with rest, you can keep anxiety at manageable levels.

Remember, no method works instantly. Managing anxiety is about consistent practice—reminding yourself to breathe deeply, taking a pause instead of rushing, and reframing thoughts to be realistic rather than catastrophic. Gradually, your mind learns a calmer pattern, and overthinking loosens its grip. In the next chapter, we will explore **mindfulness and focus strategies** in greater depth, adding another powerful layer to your ability to handle life's ups and downs with clarity and confidence.

Chapter 12: Mindfulness and Focus Strategies

Introduction

In our fast-paced world, attention spans are often fragmented. We jump from one thought to the next, check our phones constantly, and rarely experience true stillness. This relentless mental activity can fuel overthinking because we never fully rest in the present moment. Mindfulness offers a way out. By focusing on the "now" instead of the "what if" or "why did," you can train your mind to remain calm and steady—even when life gets hectic.

This chapter will dig deeper into what mindfulness really means and how you can develop focus skills. We will cover various techniques, from basic breath observation to everyday mindfulness in routine tasks. Our goal is to give you practical tools that bring clarity to your mind, reduce mental clutter, and improve how you approach each day.

---

1. What Is Mindfulness?

Mindfulness is the practice of paying full attention to the present moment, noticing thoughts, feelings, and sensations without judgment. Imagine your mind as a sky, and thoughts as passing clouds. Mindfulness teaches you to observe these clouds rather than chase or fight them. Overthinking often happens when you chase every cloud, analyzing it to no end. Mindfulness says, "Let them pass."

Core Principles of Mindfulness

1. **Presence**: Staying in the here and now, rather than thinking about the past or future.
2. **Non-Judgment**: Accepting that thoughts and emotions come and go naturally. You do not label them as "good" or "bad."

3. **Gentleness**: Treating your wandering mind kindly. If you drift off into worry, gently bring your attention back to the present.

---

2. The Benefits of Mindfulness for Overthinking

Mindfulness interrupts the cycle of repetitive thoughts by refocusing your attention on what is happening right now. If your thoughts wander to a mistake you made last week or a scary event next month, you can notice the drift and bring your awareness back to your current activity—like your breathing or your surroundings. Over time, this practice strengthens your mental muscles, making it easier to avoid long spells of overthinking.

Additional Perks of Mindfulness

- **Reduced Stress**: It lowers the body's stress response, calming your nervous system.
- **Improved Emotional Control**: You become better at responding to emotions rather than reacting blindly.
- **Greater Clarity**: With less mental chatter, you can see problems more objectively, leading to better decisions.
- **Enhanced Well-Being**: Mindfulness is linked to feelings of peace, gratitude, and general happiness.

---

3. Basic Mindfulness Meditation

While mindfulness can be practiced anywhere, many people start with a simple seated meditation to learn the basics. Think of it as a training ground for your attention.

How to Practice

1. **Find a Comfortable Spot**: Sit on a chair or cushion with your back upright but not rigid.

2. **Set a Timer**: Begin with 5 minutes, gradually working up to 10, 15, or even 20 minutes.
3. **Focus on Your Breath**: Notice the inhale and exhale. Feel the air move through your nose or the rise and fall of your chest.
4. **Observe Thoughts**: Your mind will wander—that is normal. Each time you catch it drifting, gently bring it back to the breath.
5. **No Judgment**: Do not scold yourself for losing focus. Simply notice that it happened and return to breathing.

As you build consistency, you may find your concentration improving and your thoughts quieting more quickly.

---

4. Everyday Mindfulness

You do not have to set aside a special time to benefit from mindfulness. The goal is to weave mindful awareness into your daily life. By doing so, you break the habit of living on "auto-pilot," which often leads to unconscious overthinking.

Ideas for Daily Mindfulness

1. **Mindful Eating**: Pay close attention to each bite—taste, texture, smell. Put your phone aside and truly experience your meal.
2. **Mindful Walking**: Notice your steps, the feel of the ground under your feet, and the rhythm of your breathing. If your mind drifts to worries, guide it back to your walk.
3. **Mindful Shower**: Tune into the water's temperature and how it feels on your skin. Listen to the sound of water hitting the tub.
4. **Mindful Conversations**: When talking to someone, give them your full attention. Notice their tone of voice, facial expressions, and body language.

Each of these small exercises helps you practice presence, breaking the cycle of mental wandering and repetitive thoughts.

---

5. Overcoming Obstacles to Mindfulness

Many people struggle with mindfulness at first. Common barriers include a restless mind, doubts about whether it "works," and simply feeling too busy. Recognizing these hurdles can help you address them.

5.1 Restless Mind

If you are used to constant activity, sitting quietly with your thoughts can feel uncomfortable. Start small—a minute or two—and gradually extend the time. Restlessness often decreases as you become familiar with the practice.

5.2 Doubts About Effectiveness

Mindfulness is not a quick fix that erases all worries overnight. It is more like building a new habit for how you respond to thoughts. Give it consistent practice for a few weeks and track small changes in your mood, focus, or stress levels. You might be pleasantly surprised.

5.3 "Too Busy" Mindset

Ironically, the busier you are, the more you may benefit from mindfulness. Even taking a few mindful breaths before switching tasks can provide mini mental resets throughout the day. Look for small windows—waiting in line, walking to the car—and turn them into mindfulness moments.

---

6. Deepening Your Mindfulness Practice

If you have tried basic mindfulness and like the results, you can explore more advanced techniques to further develop focus and reduce overthinking.

6.1 Body Scan Meditation

A body scan involves mentally moving through each part of your body, noticing sensations without trying to change them. Start at your feet and move up to your head. This practice helps you become more aware of tension or discomfort, which can signal when stress is building. Letting those tight spots relax can prevent anxious loops from forming.

6.2 Loving-Kindness Meditation

Also called "metta" meditation, this approach focuses on sending goodwill and compassion first to yourself, then to loved ones, acquaintances, and even difficult people. By cultivating warmth and acceptance, you reduce negative self-talk and lessen overthinking about social conflicts or regrets.

6.3 Guided Mindfulness Apps or Classes

Many apps offer guided meditations that can keep you on track, especially if you find it hard to sit in silence. Local community centers or wellness studios sometimes hold mindfulness classes, providing group support and expert advice.

---

7. Focus Strategies to Reduce Mental Clutter

Mindfulness is one side of the coin—learning to be present and non-judgmental. The other side is focus: training your mind to stay on a chosen task without wandering. Overthinking often happens when the mind leaps from one worry to another, never staying with the job at hand.

7.1 Single-Tasking

Modern culture often praises multitasking, yet trying to do many things at once can increase stress and confusion. Instead, try single-tasking:

- Identify what you need to do (e.g., writing a report, doing a chore).
- Eliminate or minimize distractions (phone, extra browser tabs).
- Devote a set block of time to just that task.
- If your mind drifts, gently bring it back to the task, similar to meditation.

7.2 The Pomodoro Technique

This popular method combines focused work with planned breaks:

1. Choose a task and set a timer for 25 minutes (a "Pomodoro").
2. Work solely on that task for the 25 minutes.
3. When the timer goes off, take a 5-minute break. Move, stretch, or rest your eyes.
4. After four Pomodoros, take a longer break of 15–30 minutes.

Using Pomodoros can boost productivity without the stress that leads to overthinking. It also encourages you to break big tasks into manageable sprints.

---

8. Digital Minimalism and Focus

Screens and constant notifications can be a main source of mental fragmentation, driving the mind to jump from one concern to another. Adopting a more minimal approach to technology can protect your focus and reduce overthinking.

8.1 Notification Control

Turn off non-essential notifications. Decide which apps really need to alert you immediately. Many times, a quick check once or twice a day is enough for email or social media.

8.2 Screen-Free Zones or Times

Create certain "tech-free" spots in your home—like the dinner table or bedroom—and certain times—like the first hour in the morning or last hour before bed. This gives your mind breaks from digital stimulation.

8.3 Mindful Browsing

When you pick up your phone or open your laptop, pause and ask: "What do I intend to do?" This simple question can prevent aimless scrolling. If you catch yourself opening social media without purpose, close it until you have a specific reason to use it.

9. Mindfulness at Work or School

Mindfulness and focus are not just for home or personal time. You can apply these principles in the office or classroom to battle overthinking and boost performance.

9.1 Mindful Transitions

Between tasks or classes, take a brief moment to reset—close your eyes, take a slow breath. This helps you leave behind the previous activity and approach the next one with fresh focus.

9.2 Desk Arrangements

Keep your workspace organized. Clutter can pull your attention away, feeding small distractions. A simple, neat setup supports a calmer mind.

9.3 Scheduled "Mini-Meditations"

If possible, block off a few minutes in the middle of the day. You can use an empty conference room or a quiet corner to practice a short meditation or do a quick body scan.

---

10. Mindful Communication to Curb Overthinking

Misunderstandings often spark anxious thoughts. By staying present when talking to others, you reduce guesswork and prevent stories from swirling in your head.

10.1 Active Listening

When someone speaks, tune in completely—no checking your phone or letting your mind wander. After they finish, paraphrase what you heard: "So, you are saying that you felt upset because of XYZ?" This method confirms you understood them correctly and can stop you from inventing worst-case scenarios about what they meant.

10.2 Checking for Clarification

Instead of walking away from a conversation uncertain about the other person's intentions, politely ask for clarity: "Can you tell me more about what you meant?" or "Just to be sure, did you want me to…?" Clearing up confusion on the spot often prevents hours of overthinking later.

---

11. Combining Mindfulness and Focus with Other Techniques

Chapters 1–11 introduced many ways to handle overthinking: setting routines, improving physical health, managing anxiety, and building resilience. Mindfulness and focus strategies strengthen all these methods:

- **With Emotional Resilience**: Mindfulness fosters self-awareness, so you catch emotional flare-ups sooner and handle them more calmly.
- **With Healthy Routines**: Being mindful while preparing a meal or exercising can deepen the positive effects of your routine—like truly enjoying a walk or noticing how healthy food makes you feel.
- **With Anxiety Reduction**: Focus strategies help you avoid mental spirals, offering a practical way to remain grounded when anxious thoughts arise.

By weaving mindfulness and focus into what you already do, you maximize each tool's impact.

---

12. Measuring Progress and Staying Motivated

Just like any skill, mindfulness and focused attention take practice. You might start strong, then lose the habit when life gets hectic. Here are ways to maintain momentum:

12.1 Journaling or Tracking

Keep a simple log of how often you practice meditation, mindful breaks, or focus sessions. Note any changes in mood or energy. Seeing progress on paper can motivate you to keep going.

12.2 Setting Realistic Goals

Instead of vowing to meditate for 30 minutes a day from the start, begin with 5 or 10 minutes and gradually build up. Unrealistic goals can lead to frustration and give overthinking a chance to criticize you.

12.3 Find a Community

Look for local mindfulness groups or online communities. Sharing experiences with others can offer new ideas and accountability. People often feel encouraged when they see they are not alone in their challenges.

12.4 Rewarding Yourself

When you complete a week or a month of consistent practice, treat yourself to something you enjoy—like a favorite snack, a small purchase, or a relaxing outing. Linking your new habit with a sense of reward can reinforce it.

---

13. Conclusion

Mindfulness and focus strategies go straight to the heart of overthinking by teaching you to rest your attention in the present. Rather than getting lost in "what ifs" or regrets, you gently guide your mind back to right here, right now. Over time, this rewires your mental habits, making you less vulnerable to anxious spirals.

Whether you do basic breath observation for five minutes in the morning or practice mindful listening during conversations, each moment of awareness strengthens your ability to resist overthinking. Pair these strategies with the other tools from earlier chapters—healthy routines, physical self-care, and strong emotional coping skills—and you create a balanced, powerful defense against mental clutter.

Moving forward, remember that mindfulness is not a one-time fix but a lifelong skill. You can practice it in the simplest tasks: drinking water, brushing your teeth, or speaking to a friend. The more you practice, the more natural it becomes, and the more peaceful your everyday experience grows. Soon, you will find that overthinking appears less frequently, leaving you with a calmer mind and a clearer path to enjoying life as it unfolds in each present moment.

Chapter 13: Communication Skills to Share and Unburden

Introduction

Overthinking is often fueled by keeping too many worries inside your head. When problems, doubts, or fears go unspoken, they can grow larger in your mind and lead to mental loops that are hard to break. By learning to communicate effectively, you can unload some of this inner pressure and find clarity. Sharing your concerns—whether with friends, family, colleagues, or a professional—helps you see issues from a new angle and realize you are not alone. This chapter will explore how communication skills can reduce overthinking, the barriers that keep us from sharing, and practical tips for opening up in healthy, productive ways.

---

1. Why Communication Helps With Overthinking

1.1 Venting vs. Bottling Up

When you "bottle up" your concerns, you are keeping them locked inside. Over time, they can become jumbled, exaggerated, or misunderstood, leading to bigger worries than are necessary. Simply talking aloud about your concerns—sometimes called venting—can let some of this tension out. Like releasing air from a balloon before it bursts, communication can relieve mental pressure and restore calm.

1.2 Gaining Perspective

Overthinking often distorts your view of reality. Talking to another person provides fresh eyes on your situation. They might highlight facts you are overlooking or point out that you are being too hard on yourself. Sometimes, a friend might even share a similar experience, helping you realize your concern is not so unusual.

1.3 Feeling Supported

One of the worst parts of overthinking is feeling like you must handle it alone. When you talk about your worries, you realize there are people who care and want to help. This sense of support can keep you from spiraling deeper into anxious thoughts. Even if a listener does not have all the answers, knowing someone is there for you can make a huge difference.

---

2. Common Barriers to Open Communication

2.1 Fear of Judgment

Many people worry that if they share their thoughts or feelings, others might judge them, think they are "weird," or look down on them. This fear can be especially strong if you were criticized or teased in the past for showing vulnerability.

Tip: Remember that everyone has worries and fears; it is part of being human. Choosing someone you trust can reduce the fear of judgment. Also, good listeners know it takes courage to open up, so they tend to respect honesty, not judge it.

2.2 Not Wanting to Burden Others

Another barrier is feeling guilty about "dumping" problems on someone else. You might think, "They have their own issues; why should I add mine?" However, real friendships and close family bonds are built on mutual support. You can listen to them in turn, making the relationship stronger rather than burdensome.

2.3 Lack of Clarity

Sometimes, you know you are upset or worried, but you cannot pinpoint exactly why. It feels jumbled. This can make you hesitate to share, because you worry you will not be able to explain yourself clearly.

Tip: Talking it through might help you untangle those knots. You do not need a perfect explanation to begin. The very act of trying to express yourself can reveal new insights.

2.4 Fear of Conflict

You might not share concerns if you fear a negative reaction. If the topic involves a disagreement—like a tough family matter or a workplace issue—you might worry it will blow up into a bigger conflict.

Tip: While conflict can be uncomfortable, keeping quiet can lead to long-term stress and resentment, which often fuels overthinking. Learning respectful ways to discuss differences is key.

---

3. Types of Communication That Help

3.1 Talking With Friends or Family

Close friends or supportive family members can be a safe place to start. They already know you, and you likely have some level of trust built up. A quick chat over coffee or a walk can be enough to unload some stress.

3.2 Support Groups

Groups—online or in person—where people share similar struggles can be helpful. Knowing others face overthinking, anxiety, or similar issues makes you feel less isolated. Plus, you can swap practical tips with people who truly understand your situation.

3.3 Therapy or Counseling

Professionals are trained to listen without judgment and to guide you toward solutions. This can be a game-changer if your overthinking is severe or tied to deeper emotional issues. Having a dedicated, confidential space to talk freely can fast-track emotional relief and clarity.

3.4 Mentors or Coaches

A mentor at work, a teacher at school, or a life coach can give structured guidance. They bring experience and can point out patterns or solutions you might not see. This can reduce the mental load of trying to figure out everything alone.

---

4. Active Listening: A Two-Way Street

Communication is not just about talking; it is also about listening. When you feel heard, it encourages you to share more. Likewise, if you develop good listening skills, others will feel safer opening up to you. This can lead to mutual support that cuts down on everyone's overthinking.

4.1 What Is Active Listening?

Active listening means fully focusing on the speaker rather than planning your response or judging their words. You maintain eye contact, nod, or respond with short verbal cues like "I see," "That sounds tough," or "Go on." You avoid interrupting and keep your phone or other distractions away.

4.2 Reflecting and Summarizing

Once the person finishes a point, you can paraphrase what they said to confirm understanding. For example: "So, you felt upset when your coworker didn't include you in the meeting, right?" This shows you are paying attention and care about getting the facts right.

4.3 Benefits of Being a Good Listener

- **Builds Trust**: Others see you as empathetic and reliable.
- **Reduces Misunderstandings**: You clarify details before jumping to conclusions.
- **Models Good Communication**: By listening well, you encourage others to do the same for you.

5. Practical Steps to Share Your Feelings

5.1 Prepare a Little

If the topic is complex or emotionally charged, think through the key points you want to convey. This can help you stay focused, especially if you are prone to overthinking mid-conversation. You do not need a full script—just a short list of main concerns or questions can suffice.

5.2 Choose the Right Time and Place

A busy hallway, a loud restaurant, or a moment when the listener is rushing might not be ideal. Pick a relatively calm setting and a time when both of you can focus. This reduces the stress of being interrupted or feeling rushed, which can flare up anxious thoughts.

5.3 Be Clear and Direct

Rather than hint or dance around your point, try to express your feelings plainly. For instance, say, "I'm feeling worried about how things ended last week, and I'd like to talk it through," rather than dropping vague hints. Clear honesty can prevent misunderstanding and reduce guesswork for both parties.

5.4 Use "I" Statements

Avoid blaming language like "You always make me feel bad" or "You never listen." Instead, phrase things with "I" statements—"I feel hurt when…" or "I'm worried about…" This takes responsibility for your feelings and is less likely to put the other person on the defensive.

5.5 Listen to Their Response

Once you share, take time to hear their thoughts. They may offer comfort, a different perspective, or solutions you had not considered. Even if they do not respond perfectly, acknowledging their viewpoint fosters a healthier dialogue.

6. Handling Disagreements and Conflict

Sometimes, you share concerns and discover the other person sees things differently. Disagreements can spark anxiety or overthinking if you fear the relationship might be harmed. In reality, conflict handled respectfully can lead to growth and understanding.

6.1 Stay Calm and Respectful

If voices start rising, take a breath. Speak in a measured tone and remind yourself that a disagreement does not have to be personal. Focus on the issue, not on attacking the person.

6.2 Seek Common Ground

Look for areas where you both agree. Maybe you share the same end goal but differ on how to reach it. Emphasizing shared goals can ease tension and keep the conversation constructive.

6.3 Know When to Pause

If emotions get too heated, it is okay to pause and continue later. Say something like, "I'm feeling upset right now. Let's step away and come back when we've cooled down." This break can prevent harmful words or decisions made in the heat of the moment.

7. Digital Communication and Overthinking

7.1 Texts and Emails

Text and email can be convenient but also risky for overthinkers. You might read too much into a brief response or worry about how your own words sound. Communication without tone or facial expressions can create misunderstandings.

Tip: If a conversation is sensitive, consider talking on the phone or face-to-face. You will pick up on vocal cues that text cannot convey, reducing the chance of misinterpretation.

7.2 Social Media

Social platforms can be helpful for finding support groups or encouraging messages, but they can also create drama. Public posts, likes, or lack of replies can spark overthinking about how others see you.

Tip: Limit social media for serious discussions. If you have an important topic, direct message or call the person instead of posting publicly. Also, remember that many people simply miss or scroll past posts, so a lack of reaction may not mean anything negative.

7.3 Setting Digital Boundaries

Decide when and how you want to communicate digitally. If late-night messages stress you out, put your phone on silent or use a "Do Not Disturb" feature. This keeps you from being in constant alert mode, which can worsen overthinking.

---

8. Knowing When to Seek Professional Help

Sometimes, sharing with friends and family is not enough—especially if your worries are severe, tied to past trauma, or causing major distress. A counselor, psychologist, or therapist can provide deeper help.

8.1 Signs You Might Need Extra Support

- Your worry is affecting sleep, appetite, or daily functioning.
- You feel isolated or misunderstood by people around you.
- You are repeating the same thoughts or behaviors without improvement.
- You experience panic attacks, extreme anxiety, or hopelessness.

8.2 How Professionals Can Help

Therapists are trained in techniques like Cognitive Behavioral Therapy (CBT), which helps you reframe negative thoughts. They also provide a confidential environment where you can explore sensitive issues without fear of judgment or gossip.

8.3 First Steps

If you think you might benefit from professional help, speak to a family doctor, school counselor, or a trusted friend for referrals. You can also look for mental health services in your area or online. Many therapists now offer virtual sessions, making it easier to fit therapy into a busy schedule.

---

9. Building a Culture of Openness

A culture of openness does not only happen in families or friend groups; it can also apply to workplaces, schools, and communities. When people feel safe to speak up, overthinking decreases, solutions are found more easily, and bonds grow stronger.

9.1 Encouraging Others to Speak

If you notice someone seems stressed or withdrawn, a gentle check-in can open the door. Ask "How are you feeling?" or "Anything on your mind?" They might initially hesitate, but often people appreciate the chance to talk when they see genuine concern.

9.2 Respecting Confidentiality

If someone trusts you with personal worries, do not share them with others unless you have permission. Gossip or accidental disclosure can break trust and make people reluctant to open up again.

9.3 Modeling Healthy Communication

Try to show honesty and kindness in your own communication. If you are in a leadership role—like a teacher, manager, or parent—your example can set the tone for those around you. People might see how you calmly address problems and feel inspired to do the same.

---

10. Communication Exercises to Reduce Overthinking

10.1 Daily Check-In

If you live with family or roommates, consider a short daily "check-in." It can be as simple as asking, "How was your day?" or sharing one "high" and one "low" point. This habit normalizes sharing small concerns before they grow bigger in your mind.

10.2 Letter Writing

When speaking out loud feels too intense, try writing a letter—physical or digital. You can choose to send it or not. Writing can help you organize your thoughts, making them clearer for future discussions.

10.3 "Three-Minute Talk"

Agree with a friend or partner that each of you will have three minutes to speak without interruption. When the timer is up, the listener summarizes what was said. Then you switch roles. This structured approach can ease anxiety about being interrupted or not being heard.

11. Overcoming Negative Self-Talk During Communication

Even if you have the motivation to speak up, negative self-talk can hold you back. You might tell yourself, "No one wants to hear about my problems," or "I'm just being a nuisance."

Tip: Challenge these thoughts. Ask yourself, "Would I say this to a friend who needed support?" Likely not. People who care about you usually want to help, and communication is part of any healthy relationship. Chapter 14 will delve deeper into defeating negative self-talk.

---

12. Conclusion

Communication is a powerful tool against overthinking. By sharing your worries, you reduce the mental load and open yourself to fresh perspectives and support. Whether you lean on friends, family, or professionals, speaking up builds connections that keep you from feeling trapped in your own head. Good communication also involves listening, which deepens trust and mutual understanding.

As you practice these skills—finding safe ways to open up, actively listening to others, and resolving conflicts respectfully—you will likely see your overthinking decrease. Problems that once felt overwhelming may seem more manageable. You realize that you do not have to carry burdens alone; there is relief in being heard and validated. In the next chapter, we will explore the topic of **negative self-talk** in detail, learning how to identify it, challenge it, and replace it with kinder, more balanced internal dialogue. Combining strong communication skills with healthy self-talk creates a powerful defense against the mental loops that sap your energy and peace of mind.

Chapter 14: Overcoming Negative Self-Talk

Introduction

Negative self-talk is that inner voice that whispers (or sometimes shouts) harsh criticisms, doubts, and negative judgments about yourself. It can appear as thoughts like "I'm not good enough," "I always fail," or "Nobody cares about what I have to say." When left unchecked, negative self-talk fuels overthinking by convincing you that every mistake is proof of your incompetence and every challenge is insurmountable. In this chapter, we will dive into the origins of negative self-talk, how it drives overthinking, and practical methods to replace it with a more supportive, realistic inner voice.

---

1. What Is Negative Self-Talk?

1.1 The Inner Critic

Think of the inner critic as a voice inside your mind that points out flaws, doubts, or fears. It can form based on childhood experiences, cultural expectations, or repeated criticism from others. Over time, those external messages become part of your own thought process.

1.2 Why It Feels So Real

Your brain tends to focus on threats (like mistakes or rejection) to keep you safe. Negative self-talk can be an overactive version of this protective instinct. Even if the voice is exaggerated or untrue, it feels convincing because it is rooted in fear—fear of failure, embarrassment, or loss.

1.3 Its Connection to Overthinking

When you believe you are not capable, you might obsess over decisions, assuming you will mess up. If you think you are not worthy of love, you may replay social interactions, searching for signs of rejection. Negative self-talk turbocharges worry, locking you in a loop of doubt.

---

2. Common Forms of Negative Self-Talk

2.1 All-or-Nothing Thinking

You see everything in black or white. For example: "I did not get an A, so I am a total failure." This ignores the possibility of partial success or learning experiences.

2.2 Overgeneralization

You take one event and apply it broadly. "I was late to one meeting—now everyone thinks I am irresponsible." This lumps all future scenarios under one mistake.

2.3 Mental Filtering

You focus only on the negative aspects of a situation and dismiss the positives. If you completed ten tasks well but struggled with one, the negative self-talk zeroes in on the single struggle.

2.4 Disqualifying the Positive

Even when good things happen, you find a way to explain them away. "Sure, I got a compliment, but they are probably just being nice." This keeps you from internalizing any good feedback.

2.5 Catastrophizing

You imagine the worst possible outcome. A small setback becomes a disaster in your mind, fueling anxiety and an urgent sense of doom.

2.6 Personalization

You blame yourself for things outside your control. If a project fails because of many factors, you might think, "This is all my fault."

---

3. Why Negative Self-Talk Persists

3.1 Reinforced Patterns

Each time you accept a negative thought as truth, you reinforce that mental pathway. It becomes a habit to interpret events in a pessimistic way.

3.2 Protection From Disappointment

Some people believe that if they expect the worst, they cannot be hurt. This mindset might prevent short-term disappointment, but it invites constant worry and robs you of joy.

3.3 Lack of Self-Compassion

If you were never taught to be kind to yourself, you might default to self-criticism. People who grew up with little praise or constant comparisons often develop a harsh inner voice.

---

4. Recognizing Your Negative Self-Talk Patterns

4.1 Journaling

Writing down your thoughts—especially when you are upset—helps you spot recurring negative themes. For example, do you always assume blame, or do you frequently predict failure?

4.2 Mood Checks

When you feel a sudden drop in mood, pause and ask, "What was I just thinking?" You might discover a negative thought popped up, like "I can't handle this," causing your mood to plummet.

4.3 Feedback From Others

Close friends or family might notice when you put yourself down. If someone says, "You're too hard on yourself," take it seriously. They might see patterns you overlook.

---

5. Challenging Negative Self-Talk

5.1 Question the Evidence

Ask yourself, "What proof do I have that this thought is accurate?" Often, negative thoughts are based on assumptions rather than facts. For instance, if you think, "No one likes me," look for real evidence. Maybe you have friends who text you regularly, which contradicts the idea that "no one cares."

5.2 Consider Alternative Explanations

Instead of jumping to "I'm bad at my job," consider that you might be new or facing a tough project. Rather than "I'm unlovable," consider you might not have met the right person or that you are going through a busy phase of life.

5.3 Use Logic Over Emotion

Negative self-talk is often tied to strong emotions. By pausing to look at facts, you can bring logic into the mix. Emotions are valid but can distort your perspective. Balancing them with reason helps ground your thinking.

6. Replacing the Inner Critic With a Kinder Voice

6.1 Affirmations

Affirmations are short, positive statements you repeat to yourself. They should feel plausible. Instead of saying "I am perfect," try "I am learning to handle challenges" or "I have the strength to keep trying." Repeating affirmations may feel odd at first, but over time, they can reshape your internal narrative.

6.2 Self-Compassion Techniques

Picture how you would treat a close friend who is going through the same issue. You would likely be gentle and encouraging. Apply that tone to your own thoughts. Try phrases like, "It's okay to make mistakes. I can learn from this and keep going."

6.3 Setting Realistic Expectations

If your negative self-talk stems from perfectionism, challenge it by setting goals that allow room for learning. For example, aim to do your best on a project but accept you might need help or extra time.

---

7. Practical Methods to Shift Self-Talk

7.1 Thought Replacement

The moment you catch a negative thought, replace it with a more balanced one. For example:

- **Negative**: "I'll never succeed."
- **Balanced**: "Success might take time, but I can improve step by step."

7.2 The "Stop!" Technique

Some people benefit from a sharp mental (or even spoken) command of "Stop!" when a negative loop begins. Right after, insert a helpful thought or redirect your mind to a calming image. This interrupts the automatic cycle.

7.3 Talking It Out

As discussed in Chapter 13, communication helps you see your thoughts from another angle. Telling a friend "I keep thinking I'm not good enough for this job" might lead them to list your strengths. Hearing someone else's perspective can jolt you out of negative self-talk.

7.4 Visualization

Imagine yourself succeeding or coping well with a challenge. Picture the steps you take and how you feel once it is done. This counters the catastrophic images your mind might create if left to negative self-talk.

---

8. Handling Setbacks in Changing Self-Talk

8.1 Accept Imperfection

You will not switch from harsh self-criticism to perfect self-confidence overnight. Old habits may pop up when you are stressed or tired. That does not mean you have failed; it just means you are human and need to keep practicing.

8.2 Learn From the Relapse

When negative self-talk returns, analyze what triggered it. Did you receive criticism at work? Were you feeling lonely? Identifying triggers lets you prepare better. Maybe you plan a quick self-compassion exercise for moments you know might be tough.

8.3 Celebrate Progress

Notice even small victories, like catching a negative thought in progress or successfully reframing a worry. Rewarding yourself for these moments—maybe by taking a relaxing bath or enjoying a favorite snack—keeps you motivated.

9. Linking Positive Self-Talk to Overthinking Solutions

9.1 Building Self-Trust

When your inner voice is supportive, you trust yourself more. This reduces the need to question every decision or dwell on every detail, directly cutting down on overthinking.

9.2 Lower Anxiety

Negative self-talk spikes anxiety, while kinder thoughts settle it. With less anxiety, your mind does not spin as frantically around possible worst-case outcomes.

9.3 Greater Confidence in Communication

As you talk to yourself kindly, you become more comfortable sharing thoughts with others, too. This links back to Chapter 13's focus on open communication. Feeling secure inside often leads to clearer, more confident dialogue outside.

---

10. How to Maintain Healthier Self-Talk

10.1 Regular Check-Ins

Schedule brief mental check-ins—maybe morning and night—to ask, "How am I speaking to myself today?" If you notice a lot of negativity, apply a technique like writing down the main worry and challenging it.

10.2 Surround Yourself With Positivity

Spend time with people who uplift rather than tear you down. Engage with content (books, podcasts, social media) that inspires healthy thinking. This environment supports a more positive inner voice.

10.3 Keep Learning

Books, workshops, or therapy sessions that focus on self-esteem and mindfulness can help you keep growing. The more you understand about your mind, the less power negative thoughts have over you.

---

11. Special Cases: Negative Self-Talk Rooted in Trauma or Deep Insecurity

If your negative self-talk ties to past trauma, bullying, or deeply held insecurities, a self-help approach might not be enough. Professional assistance could help unravel these roots. Therapies like EMDR (Eye Movement Desensitization and Reprocessing) or trauma-focused CBT can address deeper emotional wounds, reducing the constant stream of self-criticism.

11.1 Recognizing the Need

If you find your negative self-talk is so intense that it disrupts daily life or you feel stuck in cycles of self-hate, consider seeking a therapist. You deserve care and specialized tools.

11.2 Healing Takes Time

Trauma or deep-seated shame do not vanish quickly, but each small step—like one honest therapy session or one successful reframed thought—builds momentum. Long-term healing is absolutely possible with persistence and the right support.

---

12. Conclusion

Negative self-talk is like a dark filter that makes everything in life seem harder and more threatening. It feeds overthinking, drains confidence, and can harm relationships by convincing you that you have nothing valuable to say or that others will reject you. The good news is that you are not stuck with this harsh internal monologue. By learning to recognize and challenge negative thoughts, you can cultivate a kinder, more accurate inner voice.

As you shift your self-talk, you will likely find you worry less, feel calmer in stressful situations, and communicate more effectively. The techniques in this chapter—challenging distorted thinking, using affirmations, practicing self-compassion, and seeking help if needed—serve as building blocks for a healthier mental framework. This new framework allows you to approach life's ups and downs with greater resilience and clarity.

In upcoming chapters, we will look at more specific challenges, like dealing with perfectionism and fear of failure, then move on to strategies for setting realistic goals and building confidence. Putting all these pieces together will strengthen your ability to live without the weight of relentless overthinking. With a kinder inner voice, communication skills to share what is on your mind, and the solid emotional tools you have been gathering, you are well on your way to a brighter, more balanced future.

Chapter 15: Coping with Perfectionism and Fear of Failure

Introduction

Perfectionism is the desire to achieve flawless results and avoid mistakes at all costs. It sounds admirable at first—after all, who does not want to do their best? But taken to an extreme, perfectionism can become a heavy burden. It can turn simple tasks into huge stressors and create a constant fear of failure that leads to persistent overthinking. In this chapter, we will look at why perfectionism develops, how it is connected to anxiety and overthinking, and which practical strategies can help you find a healthier balance between striving for excellence and accepting normal human limits.

---

1. Understanding Perfectionism

1.1 What Is Perfectionism?

Perfectionism goes beyond wanting to do well. It involves setting standards so high they are nearly impossible to reach. A perfectionist might feel genuine panic at the idea of making even a minor mistake. They may believe mistakes define their worth, leading them to spend excessive time and mental energy trying to avoid errors. In some cases, perfectionists even avoid tasks altogether if there is any risk of not doing them perfectly.

1.2 Signs of Perfectionism

- **Over-Preparation**: Spending too long on tasks and never feeling "ready" or "done."
- **Fear of Criticism**: Worrying endlessly that others will see flaws and judge you.
- **All-or-Nothing Thinking**: Seeing anything short of 100% as total failure.

- **Exhaustion and Burnout**: Feeling drained because you cannot relax until everything is "perfect."
- **Procrastination**: Ironically, some perfectionists avoid starting tasks unless they can do them flawlessly.

These behaviors often push people into cycles of overthinking. Instead of focusing on progress or learning, perfectionists obsess over details and imagine worst-case scenarios about how others might judge their performance.

2. Why Do People Become Perfectionists?

2.1 Upbringing and Environment

Some perfectionists grew up receiving praise only for perfect performance, so they learned their worth was linked to flawless results. Others might have faced strict criticism, so they tried to avoid mistakes to dodge punishment. In both cases, the message was clear: "A mistake is unacceptable, and only perfect results are good enough."

2.2 Personality Traits

People who are naturally conscientious, organized, or driven can slide into unhealthy perfectionism if they do not develop realistic self-expectations. They may also be more sensitive to feedback, so even mild criticism feels devastating.

2.3 Fear of Failure

At the heart of perfectionism is often a deep fear of failing. The perfectionist reasons, "If I do everything perfectly, I cannot fail. If I fail, that means I am unworthy or incompetent." This fear can become so strong that the person invests huge amounts of time double-checking and re-checking, which leads to stress and overthinking.

3. How Perfectionism Feeds Overthinking

3.1 The Endless Loop of Detail

A perfectionist might focus on tiny aspects of a project, like formatting a document or choosing the "right" font color. Hours pass as they second-guess every choice. Thoughts swirl around: "What if this is not good enough?" This mental loop blocks the person from taking timely action or finishing tasks on schedule.

3.2 Avoidance and Procrastination

When the standard is 100%, just starting a task can feel daunting. The perfectionist might think, "What if I cannot do it perfectly? Better wait until I am totally ready." That wait can stretch for days or even weeks, increasing stress as deadlines approach. During this waiting period, overthinking grows because the person mentally replays potential failures.

3.3 Exhaustion and Anxiety

Constantly aiming for an unreachable standard drains mental energy. Simple tasks become complicated. Mistakes, even small ones, can feel catastrophic. This stress can trigger physical symptoms like headaches or sleeplessness and emotional problems like anxiety or irritability—fuel for further overthinking.

---

4. Fear of Failure: The Invisible Chain

4.1 What Is Fear of Failure?

Fear of failure is the dread of falling short, looking foolish, or losing respect if something goes wrong. It can make people over-prepare, avoid new challenges, or sabotage themselves just to control the outcome. Like perfectionism, fear of failure ties personal worth to performance: "If I fail, it means I am not good enough."

4.2 Why Fear of Failure Fuels Overthinking

When you are terrified of failing, your mind churns through endless "what if" scenarios. You might think:

- "What if I fail and everyone laughs at me?"
- "What if my boss realizes I am incompetent?"
- "What if I ruin my entire future because of one mistake?"

These worries keep you stuck in mental loops instead of moving toward solutions or accepting the risk and forging ahead.

4.3 Symptoms and Behaviors

- **Chronic Stress**: Fear of failure keeps you on edge, unable to relax.
- **Indecisiveness**: Each choice feels huge because of potential failure.
- **People-Pleasing**: You might fear letting others down, so you over-commit or avoid saying "no."
- **Lack of Risk-Taking**: You dodge new challenges to remain in your comfort zone.

---

5. Breaking the Perfectionism-Fear Cycle

5.1 Shifting Your Mindset

Recognize that mistakes are not proof of personal failure; they are normal steps in learning. Recall the times you learned from errors and improved. Embrace the idea that "done is better than perfect" for many tasks.

5.2 Setting Balanced Standards

Review your goals and expectations. Are they realistic given time constraints, resources, or skill level? If a standard seems unattainable, break it down. For instance, aim for 90% quality in a first draft, then refine if time allows. This approach prevents you from pouring endless hours into minor details.

5.3 Gradual Exposure to Risks

If fear of failure paralyzes you, start with small risks where failure is not devastating. For example, volunteer to lead a brief discussion at a meeting or try a new hobby with friends. Experiencing minor mistakes—and seeing you can handle them—builds confidence.

---

6. Practical Strategies to Cope With Perfectionism

6.1 The "Time-Boxing" Method

Set a strict amount of time for tasks. For example, give yourself two hours to draft a report, then stop. This forces you to focus on the most important parts and avoid endless tweaking. It may feel uncomfortable at first, but it trains you to work efficiently without fixating on every detail.

6.2 Define "Good Enough"

List the key criteria for a task's success. For instance, to complete a school paper, you might decide the writing must be clear, follow the guidelines, and be proofread once. If those boxes are checked, the paper is "good enough," even if not perfect. This prevents constant rewriting and rechecking out of fear.

6.3 Seek Feedback Early

Rather than waiting until your work is "perfect," ask for input when you have a decent draft or idea. Early feedback can highlight areas to improve without wasting time perfecting the wrong approach. This also normalizes mistakes as part of the process.

---

7. Practical Strategies to Cope With Fear of Failure

7.1 Reframing Failure

See failure as a teacher, not a judge. If you stumble, ask, "What can I learn?" or "How might this help me grow?" Adopting a growth mindset, as mentioned in earlier chapters, transforms failures into stepping stones.

7.2 List Potential Outcomes

If you are paralyzed by "what if" thinking, write down the possible outcomes—worst case, best case, and most likely. Often, you realize the worst case is not as catastrophic as your mind suggests. And if it is, you can identify contingency plans.

7.3 Visualize Success

Balance out fear-based fantasies with positive ones. Imagine yourself performing tasks confidently, finishing on time, and dealing calmly with setbacks. This counters the anxiety that arises from only picturing negative outcomes.

7.4 Break Down Bigger Risks

If a big project or goal feels scary, divide it into smaller parts. Conquer one piece at a time, celebrating each small step. This approach reduces the sense of looming failure and builds momentum.

---

8. Emotional and Mental Tools

8.1 Self-Compassion

As discussed in previous chapters, treat yourself with kindness rather than harsh criticism. Ask, "How would I speak to a friend in this situation?" Then use that gentle tone on yourself. Acknowledge that everyone makes mistakes and that is part of being human.

8.2 Mindfulness and Relaxation

Perfectionism and fear of failure often come with high tension. Practicing mindfulness, deep breathing, or progressive muscle relaxation can calm the body and mind. When the pressure in your head lowers, you can see your tasks more objectively.

8.3 Reality Checks

Challenge extreme thoughts. If you catch yourself thinking, "If I fail this test, my life is over," question that. Is it really true? Or is it more accurate to say, "Failing this test would be disappointing, but I can study more and retake it, or I can find another path to reach my goal"?

8.4 Celebrate Effort Over Outcome

Make a habit of praising the process—your perseverance, creativity, and willingness to learn—rather than only the final result. Over time, you will value the journey and reduce the fear that any outcome less than perfection means total failure.

---

9. How Others Can Help

9.1 Sharing Your Struggles

Talk to friends, family, or a mentor about your perfectionist tendencies or fear of failure. You might discover you are not alone. Others can offer tips, encouragement, or even share their own experiences with mistakes and how they bounced back.

9.2 Asking for Help

If you are overwhelmed by your tasks, consider asking for assistance. This might mean delegating some responsibilities at work or seeking tutoring for a challenging subject. Accepting help does not mean you have failed; it shows wisdom in managing your workload realistically.

9.3 Accountability Partners

Ask someone you trust to keep you accountable for not over-polishing your work or for taking small risks. They can remind you to submit your project at the deadline rather than trying to perfect it until the last second, or encourage you to try something new without obsessing over potential failure.

10. Long-Term Change and Professional Support

10.1 Recognizing Persistent Problems

If perfectionism or fear of failure is severely affecting your daily life—causing panic attacks, deep depression, or significant procrastination—it may be time to seek professional support. A counselor or therapist can help you explore root causes and offer specialized tools to break these patterns.

10.2 Therapy Approaches

- **Cognitive Behavioral Therapy (CBT)**: Helps identify and reframe irrational thoughts tied to perfectionism or fear of failure.
- **Exposure Therapy**: Gradually exposes you to feared situations, helping you learn you can cope if things are not perfect.
- **Self-Compassion Training**: Focuses on building a kinder internal voice so you can handle mistakes without harsh judgment.

10.3 Patience With the Process

Breaking free from long-standing perfectionism or fear of failure takes time. Celebrate gradual progress. Each small victory—like finishing a piece of work earlier or trying something new without over-preparing—is a step toward more freedom from overthinking.

11. Putting It All Together

11.1 Embrace "Good Enough"

Constantly remind yourself that "good enough" often leads to success. This does not mean settling for poor quality; it means aiming for high quality without pushing yourself to the brink of burnout.

11.2 Accept Imperfection

Realize that even experts make mistakes. Sometimes, a mistake provides a chance to learn a better method. Admitting that you are human gives you space to breathe and reduces the fear that any slip-up means total defeat.

11.3 Keep Risk in Perspective

Challenge the assumption that failure is world-ending. In many cases, the consequences of failing a test, a project, or a performance are fixable or temporary. Life goes on, and you can adjust your path or try again.

11.4 Review and Adjust

As you practice coping methods, reflect on what helps you the most. Do you find time-boxing particularly useful for beating perfectionism? Does visualizing success calm your fear of failure? Keep what works and refine what does not.

---

12. Conclusion

Perfectionism and fear of failure often go hand in hand, creating a potent recipe for overthinking. The belief that you must be flawless or never fail can lock you in cycles of worry, procrastination, and self-criticism. Yet there is a way out. By setting balanced standards, practicing self-compassion, and facing small risks, you begin to unlearn the idea that mistakes define you or end your hopes. As you let go of unrealistic expectations, you also loosen overthinking's grip on your mind.

Chapter 16: Setting Realistic Goals and Plans

Introduction

After learning to cope with perfectionism and fear of failure, the next key step is to direct your focus toward clear, achievable goals. Goals offer direction, motivate action, and help you measure progress. But poorly set goals—ones that are too vague, too big, or too rigid—can increase stress and trigger overthinking. In this chapter, we will discuss how to create realistic goals and outlines (or plans) that keep you grounded, productive, and free from excessive worry. From breaking down large dreams into smaller steps to using proven methods like SMART goals, these strategies will help you move forward without letting your mind get stuck in endless loops.

---

1. Why Setting Goals Reduces Overthinking

1.1 Clarity Over Confusion

When you have a clear destination in mind, there is less room for your brain to spin in circles asking, "What should I do next?" Goals provide structure. Instead of worrying about every possible path, you follow a chosen direction.

1.2 Sense of Purpose

A goal gives you a reason to act. This sense of purpose can combat the aimless ruminations that often come with overthinking. You do not have time to dwell on endless "what ifs" because you have a plan guiding you forward.

1.3 Breaking Down Complexity

Big tasks can intimidate you and fuel procrastination. By turning large visions into smaller, manageable goals, you reduce the mental weight. Each step becomes a clear, actionable item rather than a vague, overwhelming dream.

2. The Characteristics of Realistic Goals

2.1 Specific

A goal like "Improve my skills" is too broad. In contrast, "Improve my public speaking by practicing once a week" is specific. Specificity cuts down on confusion and helps you identify exactly what to do.

2.2 Measurable

You need a way to track progress. If your goal is to read more books, specify "Read one book per month." Measuring your efforts (like tracking how many pages you read daily) prevents you from overthinking whether you are doing "enough."

2.3 Achievable

A realistic goal should push you but still remain within reach given your resources and time. If you set an extreme target—like "Become a professional violinist in two weeks" with no prior experience—you set yourself up for stress and potential disappointment.

2.4 Relevant

Goals should align with your values and life direction. Ask yourself, "Why does this matter to me?" If a goal is not truly important, you may lose motivation quickly, leading to guilt and rumination about why you are not following through.

2.5 Time-Bound

Adding a deadline helps you pace your efforts. Without a timeframe, you might delay forever or worry you are behind. A specific date or milestone helps you schedule tasks and reduces mental guessing games like, "When should I start?"

(These five characteristics—Specific, Measurable, Achievable, Relevant, and Time-Bound—form the well-known SMART goal framework.)

3. Breaking Goals Into Manageable Steps

3.1 Why Smaller Steps Matter

Huge goals, such as writing a novel or starting a business, can feel like mountains. When faced with such daunting tasks, your mind may freeze, fueling overthinking or procrastination. Breaking the goal into smaller steps gives you a clear path forward.

3.2 Example: Writing a Short Book

- **Goal**: Write a 30-page eBook in three months.
- **Steps**:
    1. Brainstorm topics and choose one (Week 1).
    2. Outline the book's structure (Week 2).
    3. Write a certain number of pages each week (Weeks 3–10).
    4. Edit and finalize (Weeks 11–12).
- **Checkpoints**: Each week, evaluate your progress. Have you hit the target pages? If not, adjust your plan.

3.3 Celebrating Progress

Reward yourself when you finish a step. Simple celebrations—like sharing your progress with a friend or enjoying a favorite treat—reinforce your efforts and prevent negative thoughts from dominating.

---

4. Making Plans That Stick

4.1 Identify Potential Obstacles

Ask yourself: "What could get in my way?" For instance, if you plan to exercise daily but know you are busy on weekends, plan shorter sessions or a different type of activity on those days. Thinking about obstacles early lets you adapt before you get stuck.

4.2 Plan for Downtime

Overthinking can creep in when you push yourself non-stop. Schedule breaks or relaxation periods to recharge. Knowing you have downtime on the calendar can calm anxiety that you will never catch a breath.

4.3 Use Tools and Reminders

A paper planner, a digital calendar, or reminder apps can keep you on track. Setting an alarm to write for 30 minutes each morning, for instance, removes the mental load of remembering your plan.

4.4 Stay Flexible

Even the best plan might need updating if unexpected events happen. Being flexible—able to adjust dates or tasks—prevents the meltdown that can occur if things do not go exactly as scheduled. Flexibility also helps you avoid perfectionism, which can paralyze progress.

---

5. Overcoming Goal-Related Overthinking

5.1 The Fear of Picking the "Wrong" Goal

Some people delay setting goals because they worry about choosing the wrong path. Remember that any clear goal you commit to can teach you valuable lessons. Even if you switch directions later, you gain experience along the way.

5.2 Tackling the "What Ifs"

- **What if I fail?** You learn, adapt, or try again.
- **What if my goal changes?** You adjust your timeline or approach.
- **What if others judge me?** Their opinions do not change your personal growth.

Acknowledge these "what ifs" and remind yourself that you can handle the outcomes. Dwelling on them only stalls your progress.

5.3 Breaking Overthinking Cycles

If you find yourself stuck in mental loops—endlessly questioning each step—try the following:

- Limit your planning time. Spend, for instance, 15 minutes reviewing your goals, then move on.
- Ask a friend or mentor for quick feedback. This prevents you from rehashing ideas in your head.
- Take small, immediate action. Physical momentum often quiets mental noise.

---

6. Aligning Goals With Personal Values

6.1 Why Values Matter

Your values are the principles or ideals you find most important—like creativity, community, health, or independence. Goals that align with your values feel more meaningful, keeping you motivated even when challenges arise. This lowers the risk of overthinking, because you are driven by genuine passion rather than external pressure.

6.2 Identifying Your Core Values

Reflect on what truly matters. Ask:

- "When do I feel most fulfilled?"
- "Which achievements am I proudest of?"
- "What qualities do I admire in others?"

Summarize your top values, then evaluate if your goals fit them.

6.3 Real-Life Example

If you value "helping others," choosing a goal to volunteer or start a community program might energize you. You are less likely to overthink or lose interest because the goal resonates with your core values.

7. Balancing Ambition and Realism

7.1 The Dangers of Overly Ambitious Goals

Goals that are too big in too little time can trigger the same stress cycle as perfectionism. You might think, "I must do it all, right now!" leading to exhaustion and disappointment if reality falls short.

7.2 Gradual Growth

Aim for goals that stretch you slightly beyond your comfort zone but not so far that they become unmanageable. For instance, if you currently jog twice a week, moving to three or four times a week is realistic. Jumping straight to running a daily marathon is not.

7.3 Checking Your Timeline

If you have a year-long goal, break it into monthly or quarterly milestones. If you see you are behind schedule, adjust. This approach avoids the all-or-nothing mindset and allows for real-life changes in availability or priorities.

---

8. Staying Motivated

8.1 Track Progress Visually

Use a simple chart or app to note each step you complete. Seeing your progress visually can motivate you to keep going. It also provides evidence against negative self-talk telling you, "You are not doing enough."

8.2 Reward Yourself

Small rewards can keep energy levels high. For each milestone, treat yourself to something you enjoy—a day off, a nice meal, or a fun outing with friends. This positive reinforcement combats the boredom or frustration that can lead to overthinking.

8.3 Find Accountability

When possible, share your goals with a friend, family member, or online group. Reporting progress can be powerful. If you know someone will ask about your progress, you are less likely to overthink or procrastinate.

---

9. Revisiting and Revising Goals

9.1 Regular Check-Ins

Schedule time—maybe once a month—to review where you stand. Ask:

- "Am I on track?"
- "Do I need to change my approach?"
- "Has anything in my life changed that affects this goal?"

This practice stops you from drifting too far off course and prevents you from ignoring a plan that is not working.

9.2 Dropping or Changing Goals

Sometimes, life shifts. If a goal no longer feels relevant or is causing unnecessary stress, it might be healthy to let it go or reshape it. Doing so is not failure but wise adaptability.

9.3 Avoiding Guilt

You might feel guilty if you change a goal, thinking, "I am giving up." Reframe it as growth. You are evolving, and your goals can evolve too. Holding onto a goal that no longer serves you can fuel overthinking and block new opportunities.

---

10. Using Goals to Build Confidence

10.1 Celebrating Small Wins

Each time you complete a step, you prove to yourself that you can take action without being paralyzed by worry. Over time, these small wins add up to greater self-assurance and less anxious rumination.

10.2 Building Momentum

Success in one area often spills over into others. If you see progress in a fitness goal, you might feel more confident tackling a work project. This rising momentum replaces the stuck feeling that feeds overthinking.

10.3 Shifting Identity

As you become someone who sets and reaches goals, you may start to see yourself as more capable and resilient. This change in self-identity weakens any old habits of thinking, "I can't handle anything new," or "I'll fail anyway."

---

11. Handling Setbacks in Goal Achievement

11.1 Expect the Unexpected

Life rarely goes exactly as planned. Illness, job changes, or family emergencies might slow your progress. Accepting these setbacks as natural helps you avoid harsh self-blame or giving up altogether.

11.2 Problem-Solving Approach

When setbacks occur, pause to find solutions:

- **Identify the main obstacle** (time, resources, skills?).
- **Brainstorm fixes** (reschedule tasks, ask for help, learn a new method).
- **Implement the best fix** and see if it improves the situation.

This approach keeps you active and prevents overthinking about how unfair or impossible things might seem.

11.3 Keep Perspective

Remind yourself why the goal matters. If it is still important, you will find ways to adapt. If it has lost relevance, it may be time to revise or drop it. Either way, you decide consciously rather than letting worry make the choice for you.

---

12. Conclusion

Realistic goals and well-thought-out plans serve as anchors against the stormy seas of overthinking. By choosing specific, measurable, achievable, relevant, and time-bound targets, you channel your mental energy into productive actions rather than endless mental loops. Breaking goals into smaller steps and revisiting them regularly ensures you stay on course without becoming overwhelmed.

As you build this goal-setting habit, you will likely notice a decrease in anxious thoughts—there is simply less space for them when you know what you want and how to get there. Combined with the insights from Chapter 15 about handling perfectionism and fear of failure, you now have a toolbox that allows you to strive for success without drowning in worry. In the following chapters, we will explore additional facets of personal growth—like building confidence, using support systems, and maintaining a balanced mind for the long haul. Together, these strategies will strengthen your resilience, making overthinking less and less of a barrier in your pursuit of a fulfilling life.

Chapter 17: Building Confidence and Self-Esteem

Introduction

Confidence and self-esteem are key ingredients for a balanced life. When you trust in your abilities and see your own worth, you are less likely to slip into overthinking. Many times, second-guessing or doubting ourselves grows from a shaky sense of self. If you do not believe you can handle a challenge, your mind starts spinning worst-case scenarios. By strengthening your inner belief, you give yourself permission to try new things without drowning in anxiety or worry.

This chapter explores how confidence and self-esteem develop, how they relate to overthinking, and which practical steps you can take to raise your sense of personal worth. We will touch on everyday habits, mindset shifts, and how to stay consistent with your efforts to feel more secure in who you are.

---

1. Defining Confidence and Self-Esteem

1.1 Confidence

Confidence is the belief in your abilities to handle tasks, challenges, or new experiences. People often think of confidence as being loud or outspoken, but that is not always true. Quiet confidence can be just as strong. It is the steady sense that "I can figure things out," even if you do not know all the answers right now.

1.2 Self-Esteem

Self-esteem is the overall opinion you have of yourself—your worth, your goodness, your importance. It involves how much you respect and value who you are. Someone with healthy self-esteem recognizes their strengths and accepts their weaknesses without feeling completely defined by them.

1.3 How They Interact

When you have strong confidence, you tackle tasks more courageously, which can raise your self-esteem as you see results. At the same time, a basic foundation of self-esteem makes it easier to build confidence in specific skills or areas of life. Together, they form a protective shield against overthinking: you worry less about mistakes or others' opinions when you trust your own worth and capabilities.

---

2. Why Confidence and Self-Esteem Matter for Overthinking

2.1 Reducing Self-Doubt

If your self-esteem is low, you might see every mistake as proof you are "not good enough." This triggers overthinking cycles: "What if I fail again? What if I embarrass myself?" However, higher self-esteem allows you to accept the possibility of mistakes without tying them to your entire identity.

2.2 Easing Social Anxiety

People who doubt their self-worth often replay social interactions, wondering how they were judged. Increased confidence lessens this mental replay. You can interact more freely when you believe you have something valuable to offer.

2.3 Taking Healthy Risks

A strong sense of self encourages you to try new things—whether it is a work project or a personal hobby—without being paralyzed by "what if" scenarios. Each small success or learning experience then boosts your confidence, creating an upward spiral that leaves less room for overthinking.

---

3. Factors That Shape Confidence and Self-Esteem

3.1 Childhood Experiences

Your early years can influence how you see yourself. Supportive caregivers who praised effort and showed love can help build a stable sense of self-worth. On the other hand, harsh criticism or neglect might create a feeling of inadequacy. Recognizing these origins helps you understand why you react to challenges in certain ways.

3.2 Social and Cultural Pressures

Societal expectations, media images, or cultural norms can impact how you judge your abilities or appearance. For instance, if your environment constantly emphasizes one standard of success, you might feel less worthy if you do not meet that exact measure.

3.3 Personal Temperament

Some people are naturally more cautious or sensitive, making them prone to self-doubt. Others are naturally more optimistic and brush off setbacks easily. Understanding your temperament can help you tailor confidence-building strategies to your own style.

---

4. Common Obstacles to Building Self-Esteem

4.1 Negative Self-Talk

As covered in Chapter 14, an internal critic that says "You can't do this" or "You're a failure" quickly erodes confidence. Repeated negative messages can overshadow any evidence of success.

4.2 Fear of Judgment

Worrying about what others think can stop you from taking steps that would actually boost your self-esteem. Instead of focusing on what you might learn or achieve, you obsess about possible criticism or rejection.

4.3 Comparing Yourself to Others

Constantly measuring your life against social media posts or high-achieving friends can make you forget your own strengths. You see only what you lack, never what you have.

4.4 Perfectionism

When you believe you must be flawless to have worth, you set yourself up for frequent disappointment. This can spiral into overthinking each tiny detail, as you fear any imperfection says something negative about who you are.

---

5. Everyday Habits to Boost Confidence and Self-Esteem

5.1 Acknowledging Small Wins

Keep track of daily or weekly achievements. They do not need to be big—maybe you handled a tough phone call, stuck to a healthy habit, or learned a new skill. Over time, these little wins add up, reminding you that you are capable.

5.2 Setting Achievable Goals

As discussed in Chapter 16, realistic goals and plans reduce overthinking and give you a sense of direction. Completing small, meaningful tasks builds evidence that you can succeed, raising your confidence naturally.

5.3 Practicing Good Posture and Self-Care

It might sound basic, but standing upright, making eye contact, and dressing in clothes that make you feel good can send positive signals to your brain. Additionally, a healthy routine—proper sleep, balanced meals, and regular exercise—supports your mood, energy, and self-image.

5.4 Journaling Positive Feedback

Write down compliments or positive feedback you receive. It might feel odd at first, but seeing these words in your own handwriting can help counter the negative voice that tries to tear you down.

5.5 Speaking Kindly to Yourself

If you catch yourself thinking, "I'm so stupid," replace that thought with something gentler, like "I made a mistake, but I can learn from it." Over time, this shift in inner dialogue can greatly improve self-esteem.

---

6. Challenging Self-Limiting Beliefs

6.1 Identifying Beliefs

A self-limiting belief might sound like: "I'm not a math person," "I'll always be socially awkward," or "People don't like me." Pinpoint which beliefs hold you back. Often, they show up as "I never" or "I always" statements that leave no room for growth.

6.2 Gathering Evidence

Ask yourself if these beliefs are truly accurate. Can you find situations where you did well in math or connected with people socially? By reminding yourself of past successes—even small ones—you chip away at the limiting notion that "I can't ever do this."

6.3 Rewriting the Script

Turn "I'm not a math person" into "I can improve my math skills with practice." Shift "People don't like me" to "Some people like me, and those who don't may have their own reasons." This rewiring helps free you from rigid definitions of who you are.

---

7. Building Competence in Specific Areas

7.1 Focused Skill Development

If you want more confidence in a certain skill—whether public speaking or cooking—devote regular time to practice. Each small improvement boosts your sense of competence. Confidence often follows demonstrated ability.

7.2 Seek Constructive Feedback

Constructive feedback highlights both strengths and areas to improve. While negative self-talk only tears you down, constructive feedback guides you toward growth. Over time, adopting a growth mindset helps you see mistakes as stepping stones, not condemnations.

7.3 Embracing Incremental Challenges

Try tasks slightly outside your comfort zone. If you are nervous about giving presentations, start by speaking up in a small meeting. Then, maybe volunteer to lead a short presentation for a friendly audience. Building confidence step by step prevents the overwhelming fear that leads to overthinking.

8. Strengthening Self-Esteem Through Relationships

8.1 Surrounding Yourself With Supportive People

It is hard to build self-esteem in a negative or critical environment. Aim to spend more time with people who encourage you and recognize your good qualities. Their positivity can counterbalance any self-doubt.

8.2 Practicing Assertive Communication

Learning to express your needs and opinions calmly can raise your self-esteem. Each time you stand up for yourself respectfully, you confirm that your voice matters. Overthinking often comes from worrying you will offend others or appear weak, but assertive communication helps you feel more in control.

8.3 Offering Help

Interestingly, helping others can boost your own self-esteem. By volunteering or assisting friends, you see the value you bring to a situation. This recognition can build a sense of worth that counters self-criticism.

---

9. Dealing With Setbacks and Criticism

9.1 Normalizing Mistakes

If you slip up, remind yourself that everyone makes mistakes. Instead of spiraling into thoughts about "I'm a failure," focus on what you can learn or fix. This shift moves you from a shame-based approach to a problem-solving approach.

9.2 Filtering Criticism

Not all criticism is valid. Sometimes people project their own insecurities onto you. That said, some critiques may hold useful information. Separate what is constructive from what is baseless. A balanced view helps you grow without letting every negative word sabotage your self-esteem.

9.3 Self-Forgiveness

If you blame yourself for a past error, recognize you acted with the knowledge or skills you had at the time. Today, you can do better because you know more. Holding onto guilt does not change what happened; it only feeds overthinking.

---

10. Long-Term Mindset Shifts for Confidence

10.1 Growth Mindset

As mentioned in earlier chapters, believing abilities can be developed (a growth mindset) fosters resilience. You see challenges as chances to learn rather than threats to your identity. This perspective guards against overthinking, because mistakes do not define you—they guide you.

10.2 Gratitude and Positivity

Regularly reflecting on what you are thankful for helps you appreciate your life and yourself. It redirects your focus from shortcomings to blessings. Over time, this can reshape your self-image in a more positive direction.

10.3 Balancing Self-Acceptance and Ambition

Self-acceptance means being okay with who you are right now, flaws and all, while ambition means wanting to grow. Together, they form a healthy middle path where you recognize your current worth and also see potential for the future.

---

11. Seeking Outside Help for Persistent Low Self-Esteem

11.1 When to Consider Therapy

If low self-esteem is deep-rooted—maybe due to trauma or constant negative self-talk—professional help can make a big difference. Therapists can guide you through cognitive-behavioral techniques, self-compassion exercises, or even deeper exploration of past wounds.

11.2 Support Groups

Joining a support group or community (online or in person) where people share experiences about overcoming low confidence can be validating. You realize you are not alone in these struggles, which can itself boost self-esteem.

11.3 Mentors and Role Models

Sometimes, seeing someone else who overcame similar challenges is inspiring. A mentor or role model—be it a teacher, coach, or family friend—can show you what is possible and offer practical advice.

---

12. Conclusion

Confidence and self-esteem do not emerge overnight. They are nurtured through small daily choices: speaking kindly to yourself, taking reasonable risks, celebrating small achievements, and learning from setbacks. When you believe in your worth and capabilities, overthinking has less space to grow. You are more willing to step forward, adapt, and try again without obsessing over every detail.

Building confidence also connects seamlessly with the topics in earlier chapters—like letting go of perfectionism, setting realistic goals, and practicing healthier thought patterns. As you weave these lessons together, you create a strong internal foundation that keeps you grounded, no matter the external challenges. In the next chapter, we will focus on **using support systems and professional help**. Strengthening personal connections and knowing when to ask for assistance can be a game-changer in preventing overthinking and improving mental well-being.

Chapter 18: Using Support Systems and Professional Help

Introduction

Overthinking can feel lonely. You may think no one else understands your swirling thoughts, doubts, or worries. In reality, you do not have to fight these mental battles alone. Support systems—ranging from close friends to trained professionals—offer perspective, encouragement, and practical strategies that help reduce overthinking. Unfortunately, many people hesitate to seek help out of fear of burdening others, shame about their struggles, or not knowing where to turn. This chapter explains the kinds of support available, how to choose what is right for you, and why reaching out is a sign of strength, not weakness.

---

1. The Importance of Social Support

1.1 Feeling Less Isolated

When you bottle up worries, they can expand in your mind. Sharing them with another person can cut them down to size. Just speaking your fears aloud might show you they are not as overwhelming as they seemed.

1.2 Gathering Fresh Insights

Friends, family, or mentors often see your situation from a different angle. They can suggest solutions or offer emotional support you might not have considered. Having an outside view helps break cycles of repetitive thinking.

1.3 Emotional Balance

Humans are social creatures. Positive relationships help regulate emotions. A friend's kind words or a simple hug can calm an anxious mind, reminding you that you are valued and supported.

2. Types of Support Systems

2.1 Family and Close Friends

This is often the first line of emotional support. Trusted family members or friends who truly listen and respect your feelings can be invaluable. They already know your background, making it easier to express concerns or revisit old issues.

2.2 Peer Groups or Social Circles

Sometimes, a group of like-minded people—a sports team, hobby club, or online community—provides a sense of belonging. Sharing common interests can ease stress and lift your mind out of constant worry. Regular meetups or group chats can be a great way to feel connected.

2.3 Support Groups for Specific Issues

Whether it is an anxiety support group, a grief circle, or a parent group, these gatherings bring together people who face similar challenges. Hearing others' stories and coping strategies normalizes your own struggles. Many find comfort in the shared understanding these groups provide.

2.4 Professional Support

Beyond personal circles, professionals—like therapists, counselors, psychologists, or social workers—offer trained guidance. We will dive deeper into professional help shortly, but it is important to note that professional support can address deeper emotional or mental health issues that personal networks may not be equipped to handle.

3. Overcoming Barriers to Seeking Help

3.1 Shame or Stigma

Some believe asking for help is a sign of weakness. In truth, recognizing you need support is a brave decision. It demonstrates self-awareness and a genuine desire to improve. Mental health is as real as physical health, so seeking help for your mind should be no more shameful than seeing a doctor for a broken bone.

3.2 Fear of Burdening Others

You might worry your worries will drag loved ones down. Yet meaningful relationships thrive on mutual understanding and support. If you always present a "strong" front, friends and family miss the chance to be there for you, which can deepen bonds. If you feel a heavy load, sharing it usually lightens it—not only for you but for everyone involved.

3.3 Unsure Where to Start

Some hesitate simply because they do not know who to turn to. Maybe they do not have close family nearby, or they do not fully trust their friends with private fears. In such cases, exploring online resources, community centers, or professional help can be a good place to begin.

3.4 Cultural or Family Norms

In some families or cultures, discussing emotional struggles is discouraged. People might be told to "tough it out" or "keep private matters at home." While respecting traditions, it is still vital to care for your mental well-being. Sometimes, you can find support outside your immediate circle if those close to you cannot provide the help you need.

4. How to Seek Support from Friends and Family

4.1 Choosing the Right Person

Pick someone you trust, who respects your boundaries, and who usually listens without interrupting or judging. It might be a sibling, cousin, or longtime friend. The key is feeling safe and able to speak honestly.

4.2 Setting Up the Conversation

Sometimes, you can start small: "I've been feeling stressed lately. Can I share what's on my mind?" If you worry about being caught off-guard, ask them to meet in a calm setting—a park, a quiet café, or your living room. Giving a heads-up that you want a serious talk can help them prepare to listen.

4.3 Being Clear About Your Needs

Let the person know if you want advice or if you just need to vent. Often, well-meaning friends jump straight into solutions when you primarily want empathy. If you do want suggestions, say so. If you only want them to listen, clarify that, too.

4.4 Offering Mutual Support

Remember that conversation is two-way. If you are leaning heavily on a friend, you can return the favor by asking about their life and supporting them in whatever they are facing. Reciprocity strengthens connections.

---

5. Community and Peer Support

5.1 Joining Clubs or Groups

Whether it is a cooking club, a sports league, or an online gaming community, being part of a group fosters belonging. You share common interests, which can lead to friendships where you feel comfortable discussing life's ups and downs.

5.2 Online Communities

If local options are limited, the internet offers a wide array of forums, social media groups, or support platforms. While caution is needed (be mindful of privacy and the credibility of advice), these groups can provide heartfelt support. People from around the world share their stories, tips, and compassion.

5.3 Volunteering

Working alongside others for a good cause can forge strong bonds. When you volunteer at a community center, animal shelter, or charity event, you meet people with shared values. Over time, those relationships can become supportive friendships where you can talk openly.

---

6. When Professional Help Is Needed

6.1 Signs It's Time to Consider Professional Support

- **Persistent Anxiety or Depression**: If your worry or sadness does not improve or worsens over weeks or months.
- **Inability to Function**: Struggling with daily tasks, work, or school due to racing thoughts.
- **Physical Symptoms**: Insomnia, frequent headaches, or stomach issues linked to stress.
- **Feelings of Hopelessness**: Believing nothing can help or that life cannot get better.

If any of these sound familiar, seeking professional advice can provide the structured help you need. Overthinking can be a symptom of deeper issues, and trained experts have the tools to guide you.

6.2 Types of Mental Health Professionals

6.2.1 Therapists and Counselors

These professionals offer talk therapy. Methods can include Cognitive Behavioral Therapy (CBT), which helps identify and reframe negative thought patterns, or psychodynamic therapy, which explores deeper emotional roots. Counselors often focus on short-term, solution-based approaches, while therapists may dive into more in-depth work depending on your needs.

6.2.2 Psychologists

Psychologists are trained in diagnosing and treating mental health conditions through various therapeutic techniques. They usually have advanced degrees (like a Ph.D. or Psy.D.) and can offer specialized treatments.

6.2.3 Psychiatrists

Psychiatrists are medical doctors who can prescribe medication for anxiety, depression, or other mental health conditions. Some also provide talk therapy, while others focus primarily on medication management.

6.2.4 Social Workers

Licensed clinical social workers often provide counseling, help connect you to community resources, and can work within social service agencies. They look at your environment, relationships, and daily life to support mental and emotional health.

6.3 Finding a Good Fit

- **Referrals**: Ask your doctor, friends, or family if they recommend anyone.
- **Online Directories**: Websites like Psychology Today (in many countries) list professionals by location, specialty, and insurance coverage.
- **Initial Consultation**: Many therapists offer a short call or meeting to see if you feel comfortable with their approach. It is okay to switch if you do not click with the first person you meet.

7. Making the Most of Professional Help

7.1 Honesty and Openness

Therapists cannot help effectively if you are not truthful about your feelings, fears, or struggles. While it can be scary to open up, remember they are bound by confidentiality and trained to handle sensitive topics without judgment.

7.2 Setting Goals

In therapy or counseling, clarify what you hope to achieve. Maybe it is managing overthinking, learning coping strategies for anxiety, or resolving past traumas. Having clear goals keeps the sessions focused.

7.3 Being Patient

Change takes time. You might feel better after a few sessions or it could take months to see deeper shifts. Consistency—attending regular appointments and practicing suggested techniques—helps you gain the full benefits.

7.4 Following Through

A therapist might give you homework: journaling, practicing breathing exercises, or challenging negative thoughts during the week. Doing these exercises in daily life bridges the gap between therapy sessions and real-world improvement.

---

8. Combining Self-Help and External Support

8.1 Balance

You do not have to choose between self-help strategies (like mindfulness, journaling, or goal-setting) and external help. They can reinforce each other. For instance, a therapist might ask you to track thought patterns or practice relaxation methods you already learned from this book.

8.2 Leveraging Support with Mindfulness

If you attend a support group, you can use mindfulness to stay present during group discussions, truly absorbing what others share. Mindful listening fosters deeper connection and helps you offer meaningful support in return.

8.3 Accountability

Friends, family, or group members can keep you accountable in practicing new habits. If you aim to reduce overthinking by limiting social media before bed, you might check in with a friend each week to report how you are doing. This gentle push can be the difference between drifting off track and sticking to your plan.

---

9. Creating a Personal Support Network Map

9.1 Identifying Key People

Draw a simple diagram of your support network: family, friends, neighbors, colleagues, professionals. Reflect on who you might reach out to in different situations—like stress at work, emotional crises, or just needing to talk.

9.2 Noticing Gaps

Are there areas where you lack support? Maybe you have plenty of social companionship but no career mentor. Or perhaps you have professional help but feel lonely on weekends. Recognizing these gaps can inspire you to seek out new connections—maybe join a local club or ask a colleague for mentorship.

9.3 Keeping Contact

Relationships thrive on regular interaction. If you realize you only talk to a certain friend once a year, consider scheduling more frequent chats. When you invest in a relationship before a crisis, it is easier to ask for help when life gets tough.

---

10. Boundaries and Healthy Connections

10.1 Knowing When a Relationship Is Draining

Not every relationship is supportive. Some friends or family members might be overly critical, gossipy, or negative. If being around someone consistently leaves you feeling worse, you may need to set limits or seek help elsewhere.

10.2 Communicating Boundaries

If a friend expects you to be available 24/7 but you need space, calmly explain your need for personal time. Clear boundaries help keep relationships balanced, preventing resentment and stress.

10.3 Self-Care in Relationships

Remember that while giving to others is important, your well-being matters, too. If you are the main "listener" for everyone, you might wear down. Learn to say "no" when you are at your limit and trust that true friends will understand.

---

11. Sustaining Long-Term Support

11.1 Checking In Regularly

Make it a habit to touch base with your support network. A brief message or call can keep connections warm and make it easier to approach them when more serious issues arise.

11.2 Being Available, Too

Support is a two-way street. Ask about your friend's life or problems. Offer a listening ear or practical help if they need it. By doing so, you nurture an environment where both parties trust each other.

11.3 Evolving as You Grow

As life changes—new jobs, moves, or shifts in personal interests—your network might change, too. Stay open to forming new connections and keep in touch with old ones when possible. Each stage of life can bring new mentors, friends, and supportive communities.

---

12. Conclusion

Overthinking can make you feel like you have to figure out everything on your own, but that is far from the truth. Family, friends, peer groups, and professionals can all lighten your mental load. Simply expressing what troubles you can bring clarity and relief. Meanwhile, the feedback, empathy, and guidance from supportive connections offer new paths you might never see alone.

Building a solid support network might require stepping beyond your comfort zone—joining a group, asking a friend for a chat, or booking an appointment with a counselor. But these steps pay off by reducing isolation and providing practical help for managing stress, anxiety, and other mental burdens. Alongside the techniques you have learned in previous chapters—like mindfulness, confidence-building, and realistic goal-setting—a nurturing environment can significantly cut down on overthinking.

In the upcoming chapters, we will explore even more ways to maintain a balanced mind, from long-term strategies for mental wellness to planning for a clearer, calmer future. Having a circle of support gives you the freedom to try new strategies without fear, knowing you have people and resources to catch you if you stumble. Overthinking loses much of its power when you know you never have to face tough times alone.

Chapter 19: Long-Term Strategies for a Balanced Mind

Introduction

Overthinking is rarely cured by a single "lightbulb" moment. Instead, it often takes consistent effort, especially after you have discovered tools and insights that work for you. By developing a sustainable plan and putting in place supportive routines, you can maintain a balanced mind for the long haul. This chapter builds on the progress we have made so far, focusing on how to integrate healthy thinking patterns, emotional resilience, mindful living, and strong support networks into your everyday life. We will explore the importance of reviewing your growth regularly, staying flexible, and adjusting as you evolve. Whether you face new challenges or revisit old triggers, these strategies will help you handle them calmly, ensuring overthinking does not creep back in as an unwanted habit.

---

1. Embracing Progress as a Lifelong Journey

1.1 Moving Beyond Quick Fixes

Many people hope for an overnight transformation—waking up free from mental clutter. Realistically, letting go of overthinking tends to be a gradual process. Short-term "wins" show you what is possible, but the real aim is lasting change. Accepting that you will keep learning and refining techniques over time helps you stay patient when setbacks occur.

1.2 Ongoing Self-Discovery

Each phase of life presents unique demands, and what worked for you last year might need tweaking today. Maybe you have a new job or a changing family situation. You might discover new strengths or vulnerabilities in yourself.

Embracing continuous learning helps you approach each shift with curiosity rather than fear, reducing the urge to overthink.

1.3 Balancing Goals and Self-Acceptance

We have talked about setting realistic goals (Chapter 16) and building confidence (Chapter 17). As part of a long-term strategy, remember to balance ambitions with self-compassion. Aim high, but be gentle if you fall short sometimes. Steady self-encouragement ensures you do not slip into perfectionism or negative self-talk again.

---

2. Regular Self-Check-Ins

2.1 Creating a Reflection Routine

A straightforward way to keep overthinking at bay is to schedule brief "mental reviews." This could be once a week or once a month. Ask yourself:

- "Have I noticed any new triggers for overthinking?"
- "Which techniques have helped me remain calm?"
- "Where do I feel I've slipped or need more practice?"

Recording these reflections in a journal or digital note can reveal patterns. Over time, you will see trends in your thinking, allowing you to catch problems early.

2.2 Assessing Emotional States

Beyond mental triggers, pay attention to your emotional health. A rising sense of stress, irritability, or sadness can be an early sign you need to revisit certain methods—like mindfulness or journaling—to reset your mind before anxieties pile up.

2.3 Celebrating Growth

Self-check-ins are not just about spotting issues; they are also moments to recognize how far you have come. Even small improvements count. Noticing that you ruminate less than you did three months ago, or that you handled a conflict calmly, boosts motivation to keep going.

---

3. Routines That Support Mental Balance

3.1 Anchoring Your Day

Having a predictable structure can reduce mental clutter. Simple habits—such as waking up and going to sleep at the same time, doing a 10-minute meditation, or enjoying a short walk each afternoon—act like anchors. They ground your day so you do not wake up in panic about "what next?" Instead, your mind knows there is a stable rhythm, providing a sense of security.

3.2 Incorporating Mindful Moments

We have explored mindfulness in Chapter 12. Rather than viewing mindfulness as a single daily exercise, weave it into small moments. For instance, when you eat, focus on the flavors. During a work break, simply breathe and notice how your body feels. These little practices make mindfulness a lifestyle rather than a separate task, keeping overthinking at bay naturally.

3.3 Physical Activity and Health

A balanced mind often relies on a balanced body. Scheduling moderate exercise—jogging, swimming, yoga, or even dancing—releases endorphins that fight stress. Combine this with decent nutrition and enough rest. Sleep-deprived or nutrient-starved brains struggle to regulate emotions, leading to more worry and rumination.

4. Continual Skill-Building and Adaptation

4.1 Exploring New Tools

Even as you rely on your favorite coping techniques (journaling, breathing exercises, or talking with a friend), stay open to trying others. Maybe you discover creative outlets like painting or playing music calm you in ways you had not realized. Keeping your toolbox fresh ensures you never feel stuck when facing new situations.

4.2 Staying Flexible with Goals

In Chapter 16, we learned about realistic goal-setting. Over time, your circumstances or interests may change. You might need to pivot from one career path to another, or from one personal ambition to a different focus. A flexible mindset keeps you from panicking about shifting goals. Instead, you can see it as an evolution and adjust your plans with clarity rather than meltdown thinking.

4.3 Embracing Different Life Stages

From school to work life, from single life to parenthood, each stage brings fresh triggers. Overthinking might return if you try to handle a new role using only old approaches. By staying alert and adapting your strategies, you can maintain calm and confidence, rather than letting anxiety hijack your mind.

---

5. Maintaining Emotional Resilience

5.1 Bouncing Back from Stress

Emotional resilience is the ability to recover from setbacks swiftly (Chapter 8). As part of long-term mental balance, try to keep resilience-building practices alive. If something goes wrong—an argument, a missed promotion—process it through journaling, gentle self-talk, or seeking feedback, rather than letting it fester.

5.2 Stepping Away from Catastrophizing

When stressed, it is easy to see a problem as a disaster. Challenge catastrophic thoughts quickly:

- "Is this truly the end of the world?"
- "Have I survived similar situations before?"
- "What is the most realistic outcome?"
  This helps you avoid slipping back into negative thinking loops that feed overthinking.

5.3 Replenishing Emotional "Fuel"

Resilience also depends on rest and joy. Schedule downtime to do activities purely for pleasure—reading, listening to music, or gardening. Spend time with supportive friends. These are not distractions; they refuel your emotional energy so you can handle life's demands without tipping into worry.

---

6. Revisiting Support Systems

6.1 Keeping Connections Fresh

From Chapter 18, we know how vital support networks are. Over time, relationships can wane if neglected. Make an effort to check in with friends or mentors regularly. If someone moves away or your life changes, consider joining a new club or group. Keeping a lively social circle is a defense against isolation and obsessive thoughts.

6.2 Knowing When to Seek Help Again

Life events, such as a major loss or health issues, can trigger intense mental strain. If you notice yourself returning to patterns of overthinking that you cannot control, seeking professional help again is wise. Therapy is not a one-time deal; revisiting it or joining a new support group can help you navigate fresh challenges before they worsen.

6.3 Guiding Others

One surprising benefit of building strong coping skills is that you can support friends or family going through overthinking. By guiding them with empathy and sharing some techniques that worked for you, you reinforce your own progress. Teaching often deepens your understanding and commitment.

---

7. Balancing Work and Personal Life

7.1 Setting Boundaries

Jobs and personal responsibilities can overlap, creating stress that fosters overthinking. Learn to set boundaries: for example, turn off work notifications after dinner or keep weekends free for family and rest. Clear limits help you recharge and reduce worry about tasks you cannot handle at that moment.

7.2 Scheduling "White Space"

Instead of packing every hour with tasks, leave open slots in your calendar. This "white space" allows for breaks or unexpected needs without causing your schedule to collapse. It also gives your mind a chance to wander productively or decompress, which prevents mental overload.

7.3 Reflecting on Work Alignment

Over time, ask yourself whether your job or personal projects align with your values (Chapter 16). A mismatch can create ongoing stress and lead to daily rumination about "what am I doing with my life?" Realigning work with personal meaning can drastically reduce that sense of aimless worry.

---

8. Fostering a Positive Mindset Through Gratitude

8.1 The Science of Gratitude

Studies suggest that regularly noting what you are grateful for can lift mood and reduce stress. It shifts focus from negative thoughts to positive aspects of life. This does not mean ignoring genuine problems; rather, it balances your mental perspective.

8.2 Simple Gratitude Practices

- **Daily Gratitude Lists**: Write three things you appreciate each morning or night.
- **Thank-You Notes**: Send a brief message to a friend, mentor, or colleague expressing thanks for something small.
- **Mindful Appreciation**: While doing tasks (like washing dishes), think about what that activity provides—clean dishes, a comfortable home, or nourishment.

8.3 How Gratitude Counters Overthinking

Overthinking thrives on fear or negative assumptions. Gratitude highlights safety and abundance, reminding you not everything is a crisis. When you notice blessings, large or small, you ground yourself in a healthier mental space that discourages anxious loops.

---

9. Handling Relapses in Overthinking

9.1 Recognizing Early Warning Signs

A relapse might start with small signals: you have trouble sleeping because of swirling thoughts, or you replay a minor incident many times. Catching these hints early gives you a chance to reapply coping techniques—like journaling concerns or using breathing exercises—before worry dominates.

9.2 Revisit Core Strategies

If a setback hits, review your mental toolkit. Ask:

- "Am I still practicing mindfulness?"
- "Have I let my routines slip?"
- "When was the last time I checked in with a friend or mentor?"
  Often, a relapse can happen because one or more pillars of your balanced mindset have been neglected.

9.3 Practice Self-Forgiveness

Be kind to yourself if you backslide. Overthinking is a habit that may resurface under stress. Self-blame only adds more negative thoughts. Instead, treat it as a reminder to renew your efforts. You managed to reduce overthinking before—you can do it again.

---

10. Keeping a Growth Mindset Alive

10.1 Continual Learning

A growth mindset (see previous chapters) sees skills and emotional strength as flexible rather than fixed. You are always evolving. Read new books, attend workshops, or explore online courses that inspire you to grow in personal or professional ways. This keeps your brain curious and engaged, leaving less room for negativity.

10.2 Turning Challenges into Opportunities

When faced with a fresh problem—maybe a complicated project at work or a personal conflict—ask how this could help you refine your skills or understanding. Viewing challenges as lessons reframes them from "threats" to "stepping stones," making overthinking less likely.

10.3 Sharing Your Journey

If you have found meaningful ways to improve your mental balance, consider mentoring someone else—perhaps a younger colleague or a friend in need. Explaining your methods or discussing your journey publicly (like writing a blog post) can solidify your mindset, reminding you of your progress and potential.

---

11. Periodic Re-Evaluation of Life Priorities

11.1 Why Re-Evaluation Matters

Over time, your priorities change. Perhaps family responsibilities grow, or a passion for a new hobby emerges. Without re-evaluation, you might cling to outdated goals or obligations that breed frustration and overthinking.

11.2 Conducting a Personal Audit

Ask yourself each year or season:

- "Which areas of my life are fulfilling?"
- "What drains me more than it benefits me?"
- "Do my routines still align with my values and goals?"
  Adjust accordingly—sometimes that means letting go of certain tasks or taking on new challenges to keep life balanced and purposeful.

11.3 Handling Emotional Attachments

You might be emotionally attached to certain projects or relationships that no longer serve you. Moving on can be bittersweet. Practice self-compassion and remind yourself that making room for growth is essential to keep anxiety in check. Clinging to old patterns out of fear often leads back to overthinking.

---

12. Conclusion

Adopting a calmer, more balanced mindset is not a one-time fix, but a continuous endeavor. Overthinking habits can fade significantly when you blend mindful living, supportive relationships, healthy routines, and a growth-oriented perspective. Each step—be it reviewing your triggers, revisiting therapy, or re-evaluating your life goals—fortifies your resilience. Mistakes or setbacks become less threatening because you have multiple tools to cope.

Long-term well-being depends on consistency and self-awareness. By regularly checking in with yourself, staying open to adaptation, and reaching out for help when needed, you ensure overthinking does not reclaim its place in your life. You also gain a freedom to explore new possibilities without fear, embracing each stage of life's journey with curiosity and confidence.

In the final chapter, we will bring everything together to map out a clear path forward. We will summarize the key insights from the entire book, ensuring you can move ahead with renewed clarity, a stable mind, and a practical blueprint for staying focused and calm—even when life inevitably shifts around you.

Chapter 20: Moving Forward With a Clear Mind

Introduction

You have spent this book learning what overthinking is, why it arises, and how to handle it using a wide range of techniques—from identifying triggers and managing anxiety to improving self-talk, setting realistic goals, building self-esteem, and forming strong support networks. Now, it is time to tie it all together, forging a sustainable path beyond these chapters. This final part of your journey focuses on integrating everything you have learned into a unified approach. Whether your main struggle is with daily worries, procrastination, emotional storms, or relationship tensions, you can use these strategies as a guide for the road ahead.

This chapter will summarize core principles in a concise format, provide tips for long-term practice, and offer encouragement for the moments when you feel unsure or slip into old habits. The goal is not perfection, but ongoing growth toward a life where you control your thoughts more than they control you.

---

1. Recapping Core Principles

1.1 Awareness of Triggers

The first big leap in overcoming overthinking was learning to spot what sets you off—be it social events, work stress, or old insecurities. Notice these triggers early to stop negative thought patterns before they spiral. (Discussed in Chapters 1 and 2.)

1.2 Emotional Literacy

You discovered the links between thoughts, emotions, and body cues. This self-awareness lets you see when stress is building, so you can step in with coping methods like mindful breathing or cognitive reframing. (Covered in Chapters 3 and 4.)

1.3 Resilience and Emotional Tools

From mindfulness and journaling to positive self-talk and gradual exposure to fear, your toolbox is now extensive. You can manage tough feelings and calm racing thoughts through consistent practice. (Explored in Chapters 7, 8, and beyond.)

1.4 Healthy Routines and Physical Well-Being

You learned how diet, sleep, exercise, and daily structure affect mental clarity. Combining mental exercises with physical self-care amplifies your ability to fend off overthinking. (Detailed in Chapters 9 and 10.)

1.5 Communication and Self-Esteem

Talking openly about your worries, valuing yourself, and tackling perfectionism/fear of failure break major cycles of anxiety. Strong relationships and realistic personal standards both guard against endless rumination. (Discussed in Chapters 13, 14, 15, and 17.)

1.6 Goal-Setting and Balanced Plans

Chapter 16 reminded you that clarity in what you want helps curb aimless worry. Linking goals to your values and updating them as you grow keeps your mind engaged rather than overwhelmed.

1.7 Support Networks and Professional Help

You do not have to do it alone. Friends, family, peers, or professionals can offer insight and accountability. Knowing when to lean on them is a strength, not a weakness. (Chapters 18 and throughout.)

2. Creating a Personalized Overthinking "Emergency Kit"

2.1 Why an Emergency Kit?

Even when you feel stable, sudden stress—a conflict, a job issue, or health scare—can knock you back into anxious loops. An "emergency kit" is a simple plan listing the top strategies that have worked best for you. It should be easy to access in a crisis, helping you calm your mind swiftly.

2.2 What to Include

- **Breathing Technique**: A short script or reminder of how to do a calm, slow-breath exercise.
- **Self-Talk Prompts**: Positive phrases like "I've handled problems before; I can handle this, too."
- **Contacts**: Names or numbers of trusted friends, family, or counselors you can call.
- **Quick Actions**: A 5-minute mindfulness routine, a short walk, or writing down worries.

2.3 Storing It

Keep a small notebook in your bag or a note on your phone. The goal is to have these resources at your fingertips when panic sets in. Revisiting them regularly keeps these skills fresh in your mind.

---

3. Designing a Daily and Weekly Maintenance Plan

3.1 Daily Essentials

Aim to practice at least one mindful activity daily. That might be journaling for 5 minutes each morning, doing a breathing exercise at lunch, or reflecting on gratitude before bed. Consistent small actions prevent big buildups of anxious energy.

3.2 Weekly Reflection

Use a short weekend check-in to assess your mental state. Write or think about:

- **Successes**: Times you avoided overthinking or handled stress well.
- **Challenges**: Situations where you felt stuck or anxious.
- **Next Steps**: Adjust routines or seek additional support if needed.

3.3 Adapting to Life's Changes

If your schedule changes—new job hours or family responsibilities—revise your plan. Do not see this as failure; it is normal. Shift your mindful practice to a different time or try a new method that fits your current routine. Flexibility keeps you from slipping back into old worrying patterns.

---

4. Long-Term Mindset: Growth over Perfection

4.1 Accepting Imperfection

Perfectionism often leads to overthinking. Realize you will have days when worry sneaks in. Instead of beating yourself up, view it as a reminder that you are human. A slight setback does not erase your progress.

4.2 Celebrating Incremental Change

Confidence grows each time you follow through on a coping skill instead of letting anxiety win. Maybe you prevented a small worry from ballooning, or you spoke up for yourself in a tricky meeting. These are the real markers of growth.

4.3 Building a New Identity

As you consistently manage overthinking, you might start seeing yourself differently—a calmer person, more in control, better at handling stress. This shift in self-image further reduces worry because you trust yourself to cope rather than fearing every potential obstacle.

5. Embracing Challenges as Opportunities

5.1 Reinterpreting Stressful Events

Stress will appear—exams, deadlines, conflicts, or big changes. However, you now have strategies to handle them. When a tough situation arises, ask, "What can I learn here?" or "Which technique will help me stay level-headed?"

5.2 Growth Mindset in Action

A growth mindset means each challenge can teach you something—maybe resilience, problem-solving, or communication skills. Approaching life's curveballs as lessons, rather than threats, helps you remain curious instead of fearful.

5.3 Expanding Comfort Zones

You do not have to avoid new experiences for fear of overthinking. Gradually expand your comfort zone—try a different activity, tackle a slightly bigger project. Each time you succeed (or learn from failure), your brain's belief in your abilities strengthens, driving anxious thoughts further away.

---

6. Strengthening Relationships Along the Way

6.1 Open Communication

Healthy bonds reduce mental strain. Share your ongoing goals with friends, ask for feedback, and practice authentic dialogue. If you feel overthinking creeping in, tell someone early. A quick phone call or chat can halt a mental spiral.

6.2 Empathy and Listening

Just as you want empathy, be present for others. Listening well (as we learned in Chapter 13) builds trust and fosters deeper connections. This mutual support fosters a sense of community where everyone can reduce worry by talking things out.

6.3 Conflict Resolution

Arguments or misunderstandings can be major triggers for overthinking. Continue to practice calm conflict resolution—using "I" statements, seeking common ground, and ensuring each side feels heard. Good communication prevents small disputes from becoming big mental burdens.

---

7. Staying Rooted in Your Values

7.1 Clarifying What Matters

Overthinking often intensifies when you feel uncertain about your direction. Revisit your core values: family, compassion, creativity, freedom, etc. Ask if your daily actions align with them. This clarity keeps you from obsessing over unimportant details.

7.2 Prioritizing Wisely

Time is limited, so invest it in pursuits that honor your values. If health is important, schedule that workout. If family is a top priority, block off time for loved ones. By living in line with your values, you minimize regrets or mental chatter over "could've, should've" scenarios.

7.3 Meaningful Decision-Making

When faced with tough choices—like a career shift or a major purchase—evaluate options through the lens of your values. Rather than being swayed by outside pressure, you focus on what resonates with you. This approach lessens second-guessing and regrets.

8. Recognizing That Change Is Constant

8.1 Life Transitions

From moving cities to changing jobs or relationships, transitions can stir up anxiety. Because you now have a strong foundation, treat these changes as part of life's flow. Use your coping skills (mindfulness, journaling, positive self-talk) to handle the adjustment period.

8.2 Planning for the Unexpected

Even the best plans can be disrupted—by illness, economic shifts, or family crises. Accepting the unpredictable nature of life helps you adapt calmly. Overthinking thrives on illusions of total control, but real peace often comes from flexibility.

8.3 Ongoing Adaptation

As new technologies emerge or your personal interests shift, remain open-minded. Keep learning. Fear of failure or the unknown can spark overthinking, but your growth mindset reminds you that you can adapt and learn new skills.

---

9. The Power of Small Acts of Kindness and Gratitude

9.1 Spreading Positivity

When you show kindness—complimenting someone, offering help, or smiling at a neighbor—you create positive exchanges. This positive atmosphere can reduce stress for both you and others, limiting the environment in which overthinking thrives.

9.2 Gratitude Practice Revisited

We previously discussed gratitude (Chapters 8 and 19). Keeping it simple—a daily or weekly reflection on what you are thankful for—continues to shift the mind from potential worries to present blessings. The more frequently you notice good things, the less you fixate on negative possibilities.

9.3 Balancing Self-Kindness

Kindness also applies inwardly. If you are quick to help a friend but harsh on yourself, adopt the same compassion for your own mistakes or anxieties. This self-kindness is a direct counter to the negative loops that come with overthinking.

---

10. Reflecting on Your Entire Journey

10.1 Honoring Your Achievements

Take a moment to think about how you used to handle stress or uncertainty before starting this book's methods. Perhaps you see major shifts—maybe fewer sleepless nights, or better relationships, or just feeling more in control of your thoughts.

10.2 Owning Your Effort

Realize that no one else did this for you. You took the initiative to read, learn, and apply changes. That sense of agency is powerful. Believing in your capacity to grow fosters enduring self-confidence.

10.3 Continuing the Practice

Though you have come far, overthinking can be sneaky. Maintain your routines, keep learning new techniques, and stay open to adjusting your approach. Each day, confirm to yourself that you are worthy of a calmer, happier mind.

---

11. Crafting Your Roadmap Forward

11.1 Write or Visualize a Personal Plan

Now that you have all these tools, draft a simple roadmap for the next few months. Identify key areas—like maintaining a mindfulness practice, checking in with a support buddy, or aiming for a certain goal—so you have tangible steps to follow.

11.2 Commit to Review

Mark your calendar for a "mindset review" in a month or two. Evaluate whether your current plan is working or if you need to modify anything. This keeps the momentum going instead of slipping into old habits once the book is finished.

11.3 Celebrate Milestones

Set personal milestones—like successfully navigating a stressful event without spiraling into worry, or completing a passion project. Reward these milestones to remind yourself of your capability. These "wins" reinforce the mental resilience you have built.

---

12. Conclusion: Moving into a New Chapter of Life

Overthinking may have once been a constant companion, robbing you of peace. Yet, through dedicated self-awareness, emotional skills, supportive relationships, and well-structured goals, you have laid a strong foundation for a calmer life. You have learned that overthinking is not a fixed trait but a habit that can be reshaped with time and patience.

Going forward, remember to stay gentle with yourself. Overthinking might whisper doubt in challenging times, but you now have a mental toolkit to answer back with balance and wisdom. Keeping the long-term perspective, you will continually refine your approach. Celebrate each step, whether small or large, that brings you closer to mental clarity and emotional well-being.

No book can address every twist and turn you will encounter, but this framework will guide you. The real power lies in your ongoing commitment to your growth. When doubts arise, lean on the practices and people that remind you of your worth and your capacity to handle life's ebbs and flows. Embrace each new day with curiosity and confidence, trusting that you are fully equipped to move forward with a clear, focused mind—free to pursue your dreams without the weight of overthinking holding you back.

Closing Thoughts

Thank you for taking this deep dive into the mechanics of overthinking and how to overcome it. The strategies covered—ranging from mindfulness and emotional resilience to building confidence and using professional support—form a comprehensive map. Yet, they are most powerful when applied consistently. Feel free to revisit chapters, experiment with new approaches, and adjust your tactics as life evolves.

Remember that each of us has a unique path to mental well-being. Celebrate your progress and stay open to learning. Overthinking does not vanish in an instant, but every day of conscious practice chips away at its influence. You have already shown courage by confronting the issue head-on. That courage, combined with the lessons in these pages, will continue to serve you well.

Your journey does not end here; it starts anew, with fresh hope and direction. May you carry forward the insights gained, stepping into a life of more presence, less mental turmoil, and greater self-trust. You truly have what it takes to keep your mind clear and find focus—one steady, purposeful step at a time.

www.ingramcontent.com/pod-product-compliance
Lightning Source LLC
LaVergne TN
LVHW012104070526
838202LV00056B/5615